ENGAGE

*a youth worker's guide to
creating a culture of mentoring*

MIKE HARDER

bare
foot
MINISTRIES®

ISBN 978-0-8341-5113-0

Printed in the United States of America

Editor: Audra C. Marvin
Cover Design: Arthur Cherry
Interior Design: Sharon Page

Library of Congress Cataloging-in-Publication Data: 2012939278

10 9 8 7 6 5 4 3 2 1

ACKNOWLEDGMENTS

I am thankful my friend Chris approached me and asked if I would consider writing a book on mentoring. He simply asked me to tell my stories. At the time I was working on an idea for another book. But mentoring is at the core of my life and ministry. I am thankful to be able to speak to such an important topic in today's culture. It's been a great learning experience putting 25-plus years of thoughts and experience on paper. I want to thank Barefoot Ministries and Chris Folmsbee for the opportunity.

I would be remiss if I failed to thank the many teens and their families who have given me the opportunity to work with them through mentoring relationships. I wish I could list their names. I have learned many valuable lessons from the young people God has placed in my ministries, and the learning continues today.

I also need to thank those who poured their lives into me as a teen, then as a young youth worker, and finally as an old guy in ministry today. Joseph Valentine and Dave Quatrone were critical to my early formation. They spent time with me in one-on-one mentoring when I was a new follower of Christ. Men like Don Ferris and Ed Short helped me as I sank my teeth into my first ministry experiences. They made themselves available to me on a recurring basis and reminded me that ministry always begins at home, with your family. Unfortunately there are too many others to mention. I am thankful for all those God has placed in my life as mentors and models of how to follow Christ and be a part of his mission.

Throughout the writing of this book, I leaned heavily on my good friend Barb Delp. Without her editing eye and heart for today's youth, I would have been in deep weeds by myself. Thank you, Barb, for your many hours of aid and your keen eye for content and detail.

Finally, I would like to thank my three children, Nathan, Lauren, and Arianna, and my lovely wife, Teresa, who has stood by my side as a partner in the journeys of ministry and life. She has been an impeccable example to me of Christ and what it means to live for him. She has served as my greatest earthly mentor since our college days together.

CONTENTS

Even when I am old and gray, do not forsake me, my God,
till I declare your power to the next generation,
your mighty acts to all who are to come.
Psalm 71:18

INTRODUCTION

I never intended to become a youth worker. After attending a Catholic prep school, all signs indicated I was headed for a career in the marketplace and never look back at my adolescence. But God had other plans. Through a series of events, I ended up joining my mom on her initial visits to a church that had a strong youth ministry. On my first Sunday, a few of the volunteer youth leaders reached out to me and helped me feel comfortable checking out what the church had going on for my peer group. Once in the door, I never left. The teens in that ministry made me feel a part of them from the first time I attended.

It's nearly thirty years later now, and I have been immersed in youth ministry my entire adult life. The hearts, idealism, and vitality in young people stir my soul to this day. The next generation is always on the horizon looking to change its world. And I have found that the best place for *me* to change the world is by investing in that generation.

Mentoring is at the core of any strong ministry. If you want to make an impact on a school, a community, or a nation, it starts with the investment in individual students by enthused, caring volunteers who believe in the potentials of the ones they are focused on.

You may be part of a church that does well attracting teens. You may even have the best act in town. Onlookers may be wowed, but when the dazzle and glitz wears off, you are probably left with a nagging question: Are we really making a difference in the lives of today's youth?

Getting young people in the doors may be a great feat, but being part of God's work transforming their lives is a greater one. If we are going to impact young people today in our churches, we need to be willing to go beyond surface relationships and invest in their lives.

As Howard Hendricks says, "What you win them with, you have to keep them with." I have always been a proponent of doing youth ministry well and utilizing all that God puts at your disposal. If you have a stellar youth facility, use it for the greatest impact. If you have one room in the church basement, do the same. If you have dynamic teachers and great programs, then maximize your resources for the utmost good. But be careful what you build your ministry on and what you determine as your focus. If the most important thing about your ministry is the facility or the great programs and gifted teachers, then your reach will never go deep enough to cause significant impact in the lives of today's teens. Young people today need adults who are willing to go beyond the surface and invest their lives. They need people who are willing to address their souls and inner core. The foundation for a strong ministry is relationships. When spiritually healthy adults impart their lives to young people, the world will become a better place.

Mentoring is hard work. It is intensive, time consuming and risky. The initial payoff is not as impressive to the outside world as some alternate models of ministry. And it does not stroke the ego of the one making the investment either. But the true measure of any ministry is always below the surface. What are you doing in your church that will outlast you? If all your buildings were seized tomorrow or burned to the ground, and the pastoral vocation made illegal, what would become of your ministry? Whether you are a volunteer leader or hired gun, nothing in your ministry will outlast the investment you put in that one teen God has placed in your care.

Use all that God has given you to make the greatest impact. But beware of the inclination to fail to do the hard work of truly investing in the lives of young people through mentoring. Almost two thousand years ago, a man walked the earth who knew how to attract a crowd of people with his eloquent speech and signs and wonders. He used his gifts to influence. Thousands gathered to be in his presence. But take a casual look below the surface of his ministry strategy, and you cannot help but notice that he took time to mentor a few people. He poured his life into them and challenged them to do the same with others. He knew his ministry's impact would be determined by those he truly poured his life into and whether they would carry on his message.

Why should you invest in mentoring relationships? Because Jesus set the model for you. Because the Bible and history are littered with examples of how mentoring relationships made a difference in individual lives and societies. Because we are instructed to do so on several occasions in the Bible. Because this generation of young people longs for passionate adults to believe in them and show them the way to hope-filled and meaningful lives.

I have invested my life in imparting to others what I have learned about following Jesus and living according to his mission. The pages of this book flow from my experiences. This is by no means an exhaustive guide to mentoring youth. And you may disagree with some of my conclusions. I may do the same a year from now. But one thing is certain: We are all called to mentor the next generation.

ONE

WHAT IS MENTORING?

One generation commends your works to another;
they tell of your mighty acts.

Psalm 145:4

Young and fresh out of college, I had my first opportunity to sink my teeth into vocational ministry. Prior to this, I was an intern at a small church plant in south central Pennsylvania. But now I was trading in my intern hat for the title of youth pastor. I was going to be the one responsible for leading a small group of young people in the college town of Shippensburg.

I wondered how to start. What should I do first?

I concluded that the best first steps would be to get to know the teens. I quickly organized activities, outings, Bible studies, and midweek gatherings. These events gave me the opportunity to meet with the whole group. Yet I still needed time to get to know individuals. So I made a signup sheet asking teens to meet me before or after school, either one on one or in pairs (depending primarily on gender).

Since my budget was pretty strapped, I created the tongue-in-cheek slogan "Buy Mike a Coke." *Sign up and Mike will pick you up after school and take you out so you can buy him a Coke.* The idea caught on. Surprisingly, almost every teen in the ministry signed up. These teens were interested in spending time with an adult who wanted to get to know them better. Of course, I usually was the one breaking out the wallet and buying the soda, coffee, or ice cream. But each time I met with teens, I got to know them better.

The investment paid off. Questions about their families, interests, hobbies, and friends helped me understand more of where they were coming from and how I could more effectively help them grow in their relationships with Christ. I asked them questions in order to get to know each teen as a person, and then I allowed them to ask me questions so they could get to know me. These conversations paved the path for many of my mentoring relationships for the next several years.

At its core, mentoring is a relationship cultivated between two people—namely, a mentor and a mentee for the personal growth of the mentee. Let's break down that definition into bite-sized pieces.

First, mentoring is *a relationship cultivated between two people.* A mentoring connection has to have a healthy, growing-relationship factor as its foundation. In order for a mentor to speak effectively into the life of a mentee, the mentor needs to get to know the mentee, and the mentee must get to know the mentor. The mutuality factor is fundamental.

Consider this phenomenon. Have you ever had two people speak to you about something in your life that needed work and you found you could more easily accept the words of the one person but resisted the words of the other? Why does this happen? This is the relationship factor. Trust, respect, and connectivity exist between you and the person you receive things from more easily, while one of these factors may be lacking in the relationship with the person you resist. The stronger and healthier the relationship, the more effective mentoring can become. Ideally, it's about walking with a person and allowing that person to see your life and learn from how you live it. The human factor is a key component to a healthy mentoring relationship. Without it, your purpose, goals, and the place you want to take your mentee can seem unattainable. But if your mentee sees you as a real person who cares, empathizes, and has experienced your own bumps, bruises, trials, and struggles—yet grown and persevered—then the place you challenge your mentee to go can seem more reasonable.

Dave was a youth leader in the senior high ministry when I was a junior in high school. To my pleasure, he took me under his wing in a mentoring relationship. As a volunteer youth leader, Dave often took me out after our church youth meetings for ice cream or coffee. In those times together, he asked me questions and got to know me better, and I did the same with him. Over time, I trusted Dave and respected his voice in my life.

One afternoon our youth ministry took a couple vans full of teens to the Jersey shore to hit the arcades and the beach for a few hours. Dave and I went for a short walk on the beach. My experience over the next thirty minutes was like that of King David in his encounter with the prophet Nathan after his sin with Bathsheba. Dave asked me, "Mike, do you think stealing is wrong?"

I was a new Christian, but I had been raised with strong ethical convictions. So I answered rather quickly, "Of course."

Dave then proceeded to tell me a story of some teens going to a movie. When the movie was over they headed into a theater down the hall to get two movies for the price of one. He asked if I thought that was stealing. I knew immediately what Dave was referencing. I had been found out. A few weeks earlier, a few other guys from the youth ministry and I had done this exact thing. Dave was gently calling me on the carpet as we walked in the afternoon sun that day. Because I knew Dave cared about me and wanted to help me walk my talk as a new Christian, I took his confrontation as an act of constructive love. When Nathan confronts David about Bathsheba, he does so carefully and lovingly. Based on his relationship with David, he gently brings King David to see the error of his ways, and David repents. I did the same on that hot August day. The relationship was the conduit to speak into my life.

The second part of the definition for mentoring is *for the personal growth of the mentee.* While it is a relationship, it is important that we remember whom the focus is on in a mentoring relationship. This may seem minor, but let's look at another experience I had early in my ministry.

Shortly after I started in my first ministry, Sam approached me about his interest in working with teens. He told me he wanted to go to school to become a youth pastor like me and that he had, in fact, already completed two years at a local Bible college before taking a break to earn money. He had a quirky personality, but I told myself it takes different types of people to reach teens, and I was already spread thin. The ministry was growing, and I needed volunteers. So I gladly got Sam involved.

Unfortunately, it wasn't long before I noticed that Sam had some unhealthy perceptions of how a mentoring relationship should be shaped. While he was good at building relationships and getting teens to open up and share their lives, he seemed to expect too much in return. He became more of a buddy to teens than a mentor. His motivation was self-focused. He tried to make the playing field equal in the relationship, with mutual investment and mutual return. A healthy mentoring relationship must always be focused on the mentee. After a few meetings with Sam, I found him to be immature and emotionally unstable. My gut told me this was not a good fit and that teens could get hurt. I asked

Sam to step out of ministry and work on some personal matters before coming back. I wish I had done my homework in screening my volunteers. Sam was, in fact, on a self-destructive path that ended in a self-inflicted catastrophe in which he hurt himself and many other people. If I had not released him from ministry, several teens would have been wounded as well. But God protected those teens.

The mentee's personal growth must always be the goal. That being said, a healthy mentor constantly learns and grows and should experience some benefit from the mentoring relationships. But this should be a residual effect and not the focus. I have learned more from my three children and all the young people I have pastored than I probably learned from most adults in twenty-five years of ministry. But, in a healthy mentoring relationship between a teen and adult, the benefits to the mentor must not become emotional or social in nature. In a peer relationship, whether between two adults or two teens, the mentor may appreciate the relationship and also learn from the mentee, but the mentor also needs to be confident that the relationship is focused on the benefits to the mentee.

Far too often, unhealthy mentors have done more harm than good, particularly in adult-to-teen relationships. In my ministry, I found it necessary, after my encounter with Sam, to incorporate a staff application process and a staff ethos to help me screen people wanting to work with teens in my ministry. This process also helps prospective volunteers understand our priorities and purposes in teen mentoring and thus protects our teens from improper or unhealthy approaches to mentoring. The application and ethos also helped me prevent potentially unhealthy volunteers from joining our team.

There are four types of mentoring relationships: life on life, circumstantial, indirect, and peer to peer.

Life-on-life mentoring is when a mentor and a mentee develop an ongoing relationship that continues for an extended period of time. In this type of mentoring relationship, the mentor may speak into many areas of life, just a few, or one. My college education gave me a solid biblical foundation and taught me how to think. These were both critical as I went into ministry. But one thing I lacked was a strategy and philosophical grid to shape my new ministry. I needed help in this area. So I sought out a ministry mentor.

Don was about twenty years my elder in ministry to teens. He graciously honored my request to be his mentee. Over the course of the next few years, Don coached me and helped me grow to understand a better way to make disciples of Jesus and how to develop a healthy and balanced ministry. Though I originally sought out Don for professional mentoring, his shepherd's heart bled into many other areas of my life. He challenged me to keep personal margins and balance in my schedule. He taught me the importance of not neglecting my call to first love and serve my wife and children. And he taught me the importance of humility, servanthood, and investing my life into other emerging leaders.

Twenty years later, my relationship with Don continues. Life-on-life mentoring extends over a period of time and often impacts significant areas of your life. People expecting to stay in ministry for the long haul will need to find a few life-on-life mentors. Life-on-life mentors for teens can help them, through the transitions of adolescence and its challenges, stay centered and healthy in their relationships with God and others.

Circumstantial mentoring tends to be more short term and not as far reaching. A circumstantial mentor helps with a focused or temporary area of need. For example, other youth pastors have asked me to meet with them to discuss particular challenges they faced in ministry.

I met Adam at a seminar I taught on youth ministry a few years ago. In the seminar, I referenced my trips to Europe with teens each summer as we partnered with and served a European church in its camp ministry. Adam had never taken a group of teens overseas, and he wanted help knowing where to get started and how to execute such a trip. We met for lunch, and Adam picked my brain for an hour. Over the course of the next few months, I heard from Adam two or three more times as he had questions. Although we talked to each other a lot after his trip, the mentoring aspect of our relationship was primarily complete.

Indirect mentoring does not completely meet the parameters of the previously cited definition for general mentoring. Yet it can play a significant role in a person's life. I have several indirect mentors in my life. An indirect mentor is someone who coaches or guides through media, print, or the internet. I enjoy certain authors who help me in three areas of my life: spiritual formation, understanding Scripture, and leadership development. My bookshelves are filled with authors speaking to these three disciplines. Indirect mentoring provides the mentee with the opportunity to be mentored by people who are wise in their fields but inaccessible to the average person. It also gives the incredible opportunity to be mentored by dead guys. I have many Henri Nouwen, C.S. Lewis, Dale Carnegie, and Watchman Nee books on my shelves.

Peer-to-peer mentoring can happen between two friends or in the context of a small group where the goal is to help one another grow and hold one another accountable. This kind of mentoring relationship is helpful for teens and adults to incorporate into their lives, but in the case of teens, it can be helpful to have a trusted adult supervisor who keeps them from digressing or losing focus on their goals.

Evaluation Questions:

1. Do you have a mentoring strategy in place in your ministry?

2. Have your volunteers been trained in how to have healthy mentoring relationships?

3. Do you have a staff ethos and application process in place for your volunteers?

4. Do you do criminal background checks prior to enlisting new volunteers?

Action Steps:

• Consider the four mentoring styles mentioned in this chapter and evaluate. In which style is your ministry strongest?

• Develop a process for new volunteers to enter your ministry for mentoring. Include your philosophy of mentoring, staff ethos, an application, and a request for a criminal background check.

• Develop a staff training and equipping tool to help volunteers understand how healthy mentoring occurs.

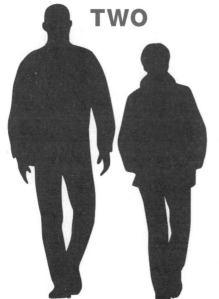

TWO

BEGINNING
YOUR
MENTORING
MINISTRY

Even when I am old and gray, do not forsake me, my God, till I declare your power to the next generation, your mighty acts to all who are to come.

Psalm 71:18

Rick was a sharp young Bible college student when he came to me look-ing for an internship and mentoring relationship. Soon he would be seeking a position in a local church to be a youth pastor. He had some prior ministry experience that included time in the local church and with Youth for Christ. Now he was looking for one to two more years of experience working alongside a someone else before being turned loose in his own ministry.

His fervor for Christ and for engaging youth in their spiritual jour-neys was admirable. And his desire to learn and to grow was immedi-ately evident in his humble yet inquisitive approach to our new relation-ship. We hit it off quickly. Our temperaments complemented each other as the relationship grew. For the next year, I tried to help Rick formu-late his philosophy of ministry and approach to youth and the church through regular, one-on-one connection points. I allowed him to come alongside me and observe me in my ministry and join me in the mission. I also tried to help him learn the need for a healthy balance between strengthening his ministry skills and a focus on personal character and depth of relationship with Christ. We regularly discussed his passions, gifts, strengths, and areas for development.

When his time was up as an intern, our relationship did not end. Rick took a position about sixty minutes from my home, making it easy for us to continue meeting periodically. Rick and I formed a bond that has lasted to this day. When Rick first entered his internship with me, I had several other ministry interns. While I spent time with each of them, mentoring them on specific ministry or life practices in the short term, Rick was the one who got my focused mentoring attention.

When determining who to focus your mentoring attention on, sev-eral factors must be considered. Make no mistake about it; everyone needs to be mentored. But you are not suited, nor do you have the time, to mentor everyone God places in your world in a life-on-life mentoring relationship. You have to be able to choose where to exert your energy.

There are a few things to consider when identifying your mentoring relationships. First, you need to determine the amount of time you think you have to invest. If the average youth pastor can maintain seven or eight healthy life-on-life mentoring relationships, the typical volunteer youth worker who has a full-time job outside the church may only be able to maintain two or three mentoring relationships of this nature.

In my first paid ministry position, I served as a part-time youth director. I was hired for twenty hours a week. To make ends meet, I picked up a carpentry job on the side for twenty-five hours a week. Despite my part-time pay, my ministry week actually consisted of an average of more than forty hours in those early years. Since I led high school, middle school, and children's church, I had to be careful about how I committed my time. This became particularly critical the year I got married. Balancing married life, my carpentry job, and ministry was a constant tension. Yet the need still existed for investing in some people outside the weekly ministry activities.

In choosing those relationships, you must consider whom God has placed in your sphere of influence who is not already being mentored by someone else. Also consider the chemistry between yourself and the potential mentees, their receptivity, maturity, and the roles certain people play in the life of your ministry and your community.

In my first ministry, I chose about five students and three leaders in whom to invest my time for life-on-life mentoring relationships. Some of your teens may already be mentored by other adults in your church or other spiritual leaders in the community, or, if you have other youth workers on your team, they may be covered by one of them. It is wise to make sure everyone is covered before double teaming one particular student. There is a tendency at times in ministry to have several people focus a lot of energy on the favorite students or needy students. Some teens are more desirable and easier to mentor. They may be stars with likable personalities or strong leadership gifts. While such teens may be important to help, we need to be careful not to over invest in them at the expense of missing valuable relational time with others.

Every ministry has at least a few needy teens. If a teen begins to require a lot of ongoing time for more than one person, that teen may need counseling by a trained professional, in addition to a mentoring relationship. Being proactive in your counseling referral strategy can be helpful. I suggest you identify the best counselors in your area—ones who provide a biblical perspective for their patients and have the expertise to help teens in particular areas of need. I maintain a list of counselors that includes personality, counseling philosophy, areas of expertise (e.g., divorce, eating disorders, anger management), and pay scales. If you do the advance research, you will be ready to refer parents with needy teens for professional counsel.

The next thing to consider in choosing whom to mentor is your heart. Whom are you naturally drawn toward? Identify the mentee with whom you can have an easy, natural connection. Please note, life-on-life mentoring relationships should first and foremost be determined by gender. Some may disagree, but I have seen too many unhealthy bonds form that started with good intentions. It is better to err on the side of conservative judgment than risk the pain or damage that can happen when boundaries get broken. Perimeters for healthy mentoring relationships are critical for protecting your teens, mentors, and ministry.

Identify whom God wants you to invest in, based on someone's role in the ministry or season of life. In my first ministry context, the people I identified included an unbelieving student, a couple of spiritually growing teens, a few ministry-minded teens, and some young volunteer leaders. In each case, an immediate connection was present, along with some kind of influence on the ministry and a need for mentoring. If you are the point leader for the ministry, it can be helpful to invest in different people at various levels in the ministry. This can help you keep a healthy perspective on the different vantage points of people in your ministry. It also can help you as you coach your volunteer leaders. If you are a volunteer leader, you should walk through these same steps to identify the best investment of your life-on-life mentoring.

If you are the lead shepherd in your ministry, you must also consider how those you are not mentoring will be mentored. Enlist others to help you provide each engaged teen with the opportunity for a mentoring relationship. It becomes necessary for you to create a strategy and ministry philosophy in which everyone can receive a mentoring touch if they desire it.

For most of my years as a pastor, small groups have played a central role in breaking our larger ministry down into manageable groups for more personal shepherding and care. This practice also makes it easier to cultivate and identify mentoring relationships because, as teens spend time with their small group leaders, trust is formed, and the potential for more extensive relationships can be fostered. If your ministry exists with a small group paradigm, you should ideally enlist one worker for each three to four students. Therefore, if you have a small group with seven teens attending, you will probably want two volunteers present to be able to offer mentoring relationships. Having two leaders in this kind of paradigm also gives the teens and volunteers more options in hopes of establishing chemistry.

Regardless of whether you use small groups in your paradigm of ministry, it is advantageous to create a team of volunteers that is as diverse in interests, talents, and personalities as the teens your ministry touches. Such diversity gives you a greater capacity to mentor more of your teens.

Jamey was a teen with very little church experience or understanding of the Bible. When I first started spending time with him, he did not believe Jesus was the way, the truth, and the life. He often joined me with his peers for a hike on the Appalachian Trail or just to hang out after school. Because of the love of our teens and our volunteers, Jamey did eventually engage in a growing relationship with Christ. My mentoring relationship became a key to Jamey's spiritual formation and ability to immerse in the local church. Unfortunately, at that juncture, my church was not an easy one for un-churched teens to enter and feel welcomed. Well-intentioned adults could not hide their disdain for our teens' casual dress and what they perceived as an air of disrespect as they entered the church building in a noisy and boisterous manner, rather than a worshipful and reflective posture.

Jamey was one of many teens in those days who did not conform to what some thought was appropriate church behavior. On one particular Sunday morning, Jamey was told he needed to wash his hands better before coming into the house of God. He liked to work on cars, so his hands were stained with grease and oil. Because of our mentoring relationship, I was able to debrief and unpack his encounter with this older man in the congregation. I was also able to help Jamey understand that this was a generational and cultural matter and that, even though this man had chosen to make appearance more important for church attendance than God, we needed to remain respectful and understanding of his convictions.

I was able to talk to Jamey and coach him in what really mattered: his heart and his continued expressions of love toward people inside and outside the church, even when they act unloving toward us. I was able to help him respect the man who reprimanded him, without agreeing with his standards. Jamey's faith relationship with Christ did not waver through his four years of high school. Despite his somewhat tumultuous entry into church life, our mentoring relationship provided the opportunity to help Jamey grow and protect him from being harmed or forming any misconceptions about church people. If Jamey had not been in a mentoring relationship, the church might have lost him to a bad experience. Jamey is an example of a student who desired mentoring and yet came to the church as a seeker.

I had a mentoring relationship on the other end of the spectrum with Burt. Burt was a volunteer youth worker, poised for helping young people grow in their love of God and others. Burt grew up in the youth ministry and wanted to make an investment in the lives of our teens, just as someone had done for him. He was a young leader with fervor and excitement to impact young people, and we found some chemistry between us. I also identified Burt as a person who would be able to help some of our other young volunteer leaders grow in their ministry skills and mentor several teens in our ministry. My life-on-life mentoring relationship with Burt focused on helping him sharpen his ministry skills and vantage point as an influencer in our ministry. Burt was a young leader who would be able to multiply my vision to impact more young people through life-on-life mentoring relationships.

Knowing whom you will mentor and how others will be covered in mentoring relationships is critical to the health of your ministry.

Evaluation Questions:

Take a timeout to analyze the following:

1. Whom are the people I should consider mentoring at this point?

2. Do I have enough volunteers to provide healthy mentoring relationships for my teens and volunteers?

3. Are there people in my church who could be teen or volunteer mentors without being involved in the weekly and monthly youth ministry activities?

4. Who are the counselors in my area to whom I would feel confident referring my teens parents?

25
*

Action Steps:

- Make a list of all your teens and key adults.
- Write down the key points you think would be helpful in finding each of them a mentor.
- List those people who are already being mentored and those who can be easily matched.
- Make a list of adults in your church who would be good mentors for any teens you still need covered.
- Begin to meet with potential mentors, one on one, to share your vision.

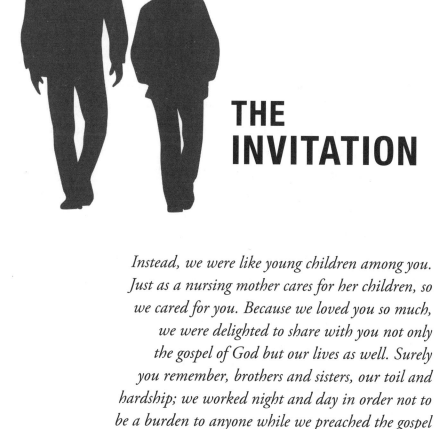

THREE

THE INVITATION

*Instead, we were like young children among you.
Just as a nursing mother cares for her children, so
we cared for you. Because we loved you so much,
we were delighted to share with you not only
the gospel of God but our lives as well. Surely
you remember, brothers and sisters, our toil and
hardship; we worked night and day in order not to
be a burden to anyone while we preached the gospel
of God to you. You are witnesses, and so is God, of
how holy, righteous and blameless we were among
you who believed. For you know that we dealt with
each of you as a father deals with his own children,
encouraging, comforting and urging you to live
lives worthy of God, who calls you into
his kingdom and glory.*

1 Thessalonians 2:7-12

The word *mentor* was inspired by the character Mentor in Homer's *Odyssey*. Despite the character actually being an ineffective tutor, the young goddess Athena takes on Mentor's form to guide the young Telemachus in his time of struggle. Walking through life's trials and triumphs together is key to the mentoring relationship. But for the Christian, mentoring has to include two fundamental components if the formative purpose of the relationship is to be a success: 1) immersing the mentee in God's story through the Bible; 2) allowing the mentee to see God's story unfold in you.

Both components are meant to lend aid to your purpose of Christ's character and his priorities being etched into the mentee's life fabric and spirit. By immersing your teens in God's story and allowing them to see God's story unfold in your life, you give them a better picture of how God can shape their lives and help them in their trials and triumphs.

Note the emphasis the apostle Paul puts on sharing "the gospel of God" in the 1 Thessalonians passage. The Bible is central to the mentoring process. The purpose for mentoring in your youth ministry is not just to build relationships with teachable teens. While this is important, you need to remember your goal is first and foremost to center your teens in the story of God. God's story provides the true backdrop for youth to understand who they are, what God has for them, and how they can best live their lives and glorify him. For this reason, God's Word should be central as it is incorporated into all mentoring relationships. One need not look further than Paul and Jesus and their constant use of Scripture in their mentoring encounters. It is crucial that you point your teens to the Bible as their source of direction and strength.

Joe was a young seminarian who worked in the youth ministry at my new church when I was a teen. He often took me to his home following church on Sundays. We spent the remainder of the day getting to know each other through activities, eating his mom's hearty Italian cooking with the family, and reading and studying the Bible together. Even though I was an unbeliever, I appreciated his investment in me as a teenager, and his efforts to help me figure out how God could become a part of my life. He was careful to point me to God as the hero and not himself. It is critical that your mentees understand that you are simply a model who points them to Christ as their provider and source. It helps to keep the Bible central in your relationships.

Paul also says in the Thessalonians passage that he shared his life, in addition to sharing the gospel. The word used for *life* in this passage is also sometimes translated *soul*. Paul has shared his very soul with the Thessalonians. A careful look at the book of Acts shows us that Paul does not spend a lot of time in their city. However, when he is there, he intentionally invests in relationships. In 1 Thessalonians 2, Paul wants us to see that he has gone beyond simply preaching the Bible to his mentees; he has invested his life. He has gotten to know them as people and allowed them to get to know him as well. It is important that we note both of these characteristics of Paul's approach because the Word of God is the substance of mentoring, and your life is the flesh that demonstrates the Word being lived out. You are, in essence, Christ in the flesh for your teens.

> Christ has no body but yours,
> No hands, no feet on earth but yours,
> Yours are the eyes with which he looks
> Compassion on this world,
> Yours are the feet with which he walks to do good,
> Yours are the hands, with which he blesses all the world.
> Yours are the hands, yours are the feet,
> Yours are the eyes, you are his body.
> Christ has no body now but yours,
> No hands, no feet on earth but yours,
> Yours are the eyes with which he looks
> compassion on this world.
> Christ has no body now on earth but yours.
> —Teresa of Avila, a Carmelite Nun (1515–1582)

One morning I had coffee with Andy, who at the time had been interning with me over the last three years. Andy and I have shared many ministry experiences together and have had several talks on ministry and the life of the youth worker over cups of coffee. The subject of modeling came up in this particular coffee conversation. He told me that the most indelible memory he had from our years of mentoring did not come from leading a ministry event alongside me or from one of our mentoring meetings. For him, the greatest impact came from a car ride together.

We were stopped at a red light, and I saw the side utility door on the carpenters' truck in front of us hanging open. The driver was about to lose some of his tools and supplies. I jumped out of my car and ran up and closed his door and then walked up to the truck window to give the driver a heads up. While sipping his coffee, Andy told me that in that moment, he saw the nature of servanthood.

My experience with Andy made me think about the importance of life-on-life mentoring and a balanced approach. To simply teach the Bible is not enough. We need to show others how we wrestle to live it out. This is why you need to be a proponent of life-on-life mentoring in your ministry. As Howard Hendricks once said, "More is caught than taught." This teaching should demonstrate how what you see in the Bible can be lived out in your daily life.

Let me take you back to the story of Joe. I do not recall how I first met Joe at church. But I do know that he understood how to work with teens and meet them where they were in their spiritual walks. As a seeker, I felt comfortable with him. I was able to ask questions, make comments, and be myself without feeling intimidated or stupid. Joe was able to figure out fairly quickly where I was in my walk with Christ and what my next steps needed to be to grow.

At the time, my mother was in the hospital, and she was dying. My father spent the evenings at her bedside. This left both my sister and me in need of extra care from other significant adults. My mom's church and pastor stepped up. As one of the church's youth workers, Joe helped fill a lot of the gaps in my life at that time. He walked with me in a life-on-life mentoring relationship, exploring the Bible with me, demonstrating how to live out its principles, and helping me see the potential I had in a life following Christ. He often challenged me and helped me see what God was doing and how he wanted to work in my life.

Being an effective mentor requires the ability to enter another person's world and assess spiritual maturity. Then you need to determine how you will help that person move forward. You need to work with your mentee to identify blind spots, fatal flaws, and areas for development. A blind spot is a potentially destructive characteristic or trait that can hinder someone's relationship with others and God. A fatal flaw is an inclination or weakness that lends itself to a pattern of sin that can trap or destroy you.

While there are principles and practices that transcend all mentoring relationships, each mentee must be approached on an individual basis to assess goals and desired growing points. As a spiritual tutor, you need to be able treat each teen as an individual. When you begin a mentoring relationship, determine the goals of your encounters with the help of the mentee. At times, you may have insights into the person's life that come from discernment and prayer that are difficult or not productive to share at the beginning of your journey. They may escape the mentee's knowledge or may be difficult to bring up at the time.

Case in point: If you are mentoring a teenage girl whose parents just went through a divorce and she tells you that she does not want to talk about her family or the divorce, you may choose not to broach the subject for a time. But you know that healing, forgiveness, and resolution will be critical steps for her to embrace if she is to move forward. For the time being, you need to discern tactics to help her progress while not discussing the circumstances she has requested to keep off limits. A mature mentor knows how to identify agreed-upon goals while also considering goals that the Holy Spirit lays on the heart to pray through and work toward.

In the movie *The King's Speech*, the sudden death of King George V and the immoral shenanigans and abdication of his brother, Edward, leave Bertie (King George VI) as the new king at a time when Britain desperately needs a leader to give them the courage to press forward and remain unified.

The only trouble is, Bertie has suffered from a debilitating speech impediment all his life. The newly crowned King George VI needs help to overcome his stammer so he can courageously lead his nation forward. In an attempt to help her husband, Bertie's wife seeks the assistance of an eccentric and unorthodox speech therapist named Lionel Logue. After a rocky start, Lionel begins to break down the walls and helps Bertie get the upper hand on his demon. In order to help the king, Lionel must help him find his voice—one that has been repressed by years of callousness during his childhood. Lionel sees the character and potential of his mentee and helps him lead his nation in this historic, defining moment. In this true story, Bertie and Lionel form a lifelong bond that is actually a life-on-life mentoring relationship.

In its purest sense, a good mentoring relationship speaks to all facets of a person's life: mind, body, spirit, family, finances, etc. Each person's sacred and secular life is one and the same since all life is sacred and belonging to God. Good mentors can identify where people have compartmentalized their lives to keep God and others out. It is true that in some instances you will only have the opportunity to speak into a particular area of a person's life. But effective mentoring has to do with walking alongside someone through life or letting someone walk beside you. Nothing is out of God's interest. Therefore, nothing should be untouched by a true life-on-life mentor.

Depending on your life experience and strengths, you will have a natural tendency to address certain aspects of life and neglect others. It is important that you identify and write down areas to address to help set goals that foster a more holistic approach to your mentoring relationship. And the better you get to know the true person you are mentoring, the more impact your relationship will have.

Note in 1 Thessalonians how Paul uses the role of parents in a child's life to show the way you approach those you mentor. Mothers and fathers tend to communicate and nurture differently. You need to find a balance between the nurturing love of a mother and the hardworking nature of a father. A mother, in this sense, can give a child the empathy and tender love needed. On the other hand, a father can help the child with the character and determination needed to press forward toward the goals for growth. Paul gives a balanced approach through his traditional vantage point of parents in childrearing.

Evaluation Questions:

1. What areas of life do you tend to focus on most often?

2. What are the fatal flaws and blind spots you have had to address in your life?

3. What other struggles have you had to fight that have defined or impacted you as a person?

4. What is different in the needs of those you are mentoring?

Action Steps:

33
*

Look at the people you are mentoring or considering as potential mentees. Determine the following:

1. Where do you think they are spiritually?
2. What practices or disciplines do you believe would help them grow?
3. What are their blind spots or fatal flaws?
4. What struggles or wounds from their past should be recognized as you consider how to help them grow?
5. In what relationships do they need to be coached to bring greater health?

FOUR

THE PROCESS OF SPIRITUAL FORMATION

So even to old age and gray hairs, O God, do not forsake me, until I proclaim your might to another generation, your power to all those to come.

Psalm 71:8

In my junior year of college, I was excited when the opportunity arose to move from dorm life to an apartment. Don't get me wrong; dorm life was amusing, and it helped me make friends on campus my first two years, but an apartment gave me new freedoms and a better environment for studying.

As part of the move, I opted out of the full meal plan in an attempt to save a little money. I decided I would cook for myself in my new kitchen. Over the next several months, my menu was microwave-friendly leftovers from my pizza shop job or Ramen noodles. Meals took on a form for instant salivary gratification. I traded the school cafeteria food for quickly nuked meals. Time and money might have been saved, but the substance and quality of my diet digressed considerably. Substance was traded for expedition and convenience.

It would be easy to make the same mistake in your approach to mentoring. Quick and instant. However, to bring substantial change to the life of the mentee, you must be committed to the long-term process of spiritual formation. The maturity of your mentees comes via the Crockpot approach. It takes time, heart, and commitment.

I have been coaching soccer for more than fifteen years. I have worked with little tykes who run around in an amoeba huddle, aimlessly dancing about and taking the ball up and down the field. I have coached finely tuned high-school-level teams who worked together as a unit—passing, moving, and playing the entire field in a calculated and synchronized system. And I have coached the gamut of ages and skills between these two extremes. The longest I have ever worked with one group of players is ten years. Starting with four- and five-year-olds, I coached and mentored these little ones to learn simple skills like passing a ball and basic dribbling. As they got older, the level of skill development and training increased to special dribbling moves to get around their opponents, tactical positioning, and passing to overcome the other team. Although the fundamentals taught at a preschool level still applied to my high school teens, what I taught the high school teens did not apply to the little ones. As a coach, you have to recognize process and maturity.

The same is true in your mentoring relationships. Take time to assess the person you are mentoring. Where is the mentee in terms of spiritual and social maturity? What are the mentee's blind spots, fatal flaws, and areas in need of development? It is also important to revisit each of these areas in a recurring fashion throughout the mentoring process. As your relationship develops, you will hopefully gain a greater level of trust, transparency, and understanding of the person. You will learn new things you can do to help the mentee map a path for spiritual formation.

Once you begin mentoring, it is important that you establish a healthy pace for discipleship. At times you may need to adjust your pace, based on how you see things progressing. You may hit sticking points or walls that require more time and prayer to overcome.

Colleen came into the ministry with a friend. She was a curious seeker not yet committed to Christ. It became clear in the first few months of getting to know her that she had a desire for a relationship with God, but she needed to overcome some hurdles before she could move forward. For some reason, Colleen had difficulty taking the first steps once she expressed interest in becoming a Christ follower. She struggled to comprehend the gospel and God's love for her. Early on, she and her mentors hit a wall in their relationships. Colleen was making a lot of progress in some respects, but crossing the line to an authentic relationship with Christ was not happening. This was not because of a lack of desire. Some deep wounds existed that made it impossible for her to comprehend the Bible's truths when she heard them. Spiritual bondage had a grip on her life.

More trust had to be established in order for transparency to grow and for her to address her pain. Her mentors spent time focused on communicating love and fostering trust in the relationship. In a few months, Colleen began to share what was holding her back. Interestingly, all of this was happening without her knowledge of how debilitating her inner turmoil was to her spiritual formation. Through prayer and love, her mentors were able to help her break through. Colleen opened up one afternoon, sharing with two leaders who had invested time with her ever since she joined the youth ministry. The sobering truth she shared was heartbreaking.

As a fourteen- or fifteen-year-old girl, she had been raped several times at parties she attended with friends. To this point, she had not divulged her dark, agonizing secrets to anyone. Instead she carried them alone for a few years. Her mentors cried with her, prayed for her, expressed empathy, and assured her it was not her fault. They apologized for the way she was violated. In the matter of an hour, Colleen shared her wounds, confessed belief in Christ, and began to make strides forward in her walk with God. Until the inner pain could be addressed, she was imprisoned by her demons.

Colleen's life-on-life mentor and other adults helped her move forward in her walk with Christ, and she began to change the way she thought about herself and others. Her spiritual and emotional growth were steady and incremental over the years following her breakthrough, largely due to the commitment of the adults that mentored her.

A wise mentor can prayerfully discern when something is obstructing spiritual growth. Sometimes, like Colleen, the mentee may not be aware. It's too deep inside. Other times, it may be a conscious decision the student is making to resist moving forward out of fear of what must be changed or given up. A good mentor can discern the problem and attempt to help the mentee move forward and grow. But, at the end of the day, matters such as these must be committed to prayer because God is the only one who can transform a heart and set a person free.

Everyone has at least one fatal flaw, or issue of some shape or form that needs confronted. In some cases, a fatal flaw may be hindering a mentee from moving forward in spiritual growth. And, in most of our lives, our fatal flaws will catch up with us if we do not learn to address them. Remember, a fatal flaw is an inclination or weakness that lends itself to a sinful pattern that can trap or destroy a person. Addressing fatal flaws in a person's life is hard work. Some of the time, a mentee may ask for help to overcome or get control of fatal flaws. At other times you as the mentor may have to challenge your mentee to address the issues. You may not always have a shared awareness of the weaknesses or knowledge of how dangerous they can be.

> **And you see, looking back, how all the plans you have ever made always have shipwrecked on that fatal flaw—on "X's" incurable jealousy, or laziness, or touchiness, or muddle-headedness, or bossiness, or ill temper, or changeableness . . .**
> C. S. Lewis, *God in the Dock*

Josh sat across the table from me at a local hot spot for breakfast. Our mentoring relationship was four years old, when he divulged his recent struggle. Over the past few months, he had delved into pornography and now felt trapped and defeated. He did not know how to get out and pleaded for help. Helping Josh with his pornography addiction was not simple. It required his ongoing honesty in a few critical relationships and several tactics to be put in place. Over a short period of time, Josh was able to gain more mastery of his addiction and see some victory with the encouragement of his accountability friends.

When addressing a fatal flaw in a mentee's life, you need to know how strong a grip the flaw has gained over the mentee. Fatal flaws exist in many forms and can flow from one's vices *or* virtues. I once had a ministry friend whom I mentored for a few years. He was a gifted leader, but his lack of tact and interpersonal skills often caused him to alienate those he tried to lead. He frequently left carnage in his wake. Such behavior would eventually lead to people avoiding him or even his dismissal from ministry posts. My task was to help him see the impact his fatal flaw had on his relationships and, ultimately, his success (or lack thereof) as a servant of God.

Many biblical characters provide examples of the impact of a fatal flaw taking root their lives. For Jacob, it is deception. For Solomon, it is an unhealthy love of women. For Achan, it is a greedy desire for money. Everyone has a fatal flaw. A mentor's task is to help the mentee identify it and map out a strategy to control it. Since many people's fatal flaws result in their demise, this is a very important issue for a mentor to ad-

39
*

dress. In cases where a fatal flaw has taken root and drawn a person into destructive behavior, you may need to point your mentee to professional help. Regardless, you must remember that addressing serious matters like fatal flaws in a person's life requires an ongoing process and not a short-term commitment.

Coaching your mentee in relationship skills is also important in helping the mentee become more mature in his or her faith. Parents and teens, peer dating, and teacher-to-student connections are all relationships that can take ongoing coaching. This is especially true if mentees have unhealthy interpersonal skills or strained relationships with other people in their lives. Unfortunately, you will probably have your share of parent-to-teen relationships to address in your ministry.

John's relationship with his parents was damaged for a few years. He and his father seemed to be cut from different cloths. His well-intentioned and authoritarian dad unknowingly pushed his son away from him. Then, when John told his parents he was struggling with his sexual identity, the relationship quickly degenerated to the point that John moved out of his house in the middle of his senior year of high school. For a few weeks, John slept in parks and trees. Communication became next to nil and the wounds, and bitterness ran deep. Mentoring John toward wholeness, forgiveness, and health was not easy. It was important that I not negate his feelings or minimize his pain.

While trying to give John a place to share, I also had to help him accept his responsibility as a Christian in his relationships with his mom and dad. As we met, I was able to suggest things he could do to show respect and God's love toward his father. Their relationship is still strained, but some headway has been made. Healing is slowly taking place, and hopefully their family relationships can be mended and John can experience healthy relationships in all areas of his life.

John needed a mentor who would stick by him for an extended time. His life is far too messy to address in a few casual meetings. Although John's story may be more extreme than that of your average mentee, it does illustrate the complexity of people's relationships and the benefit an outside voice can have in a person's life. By offering mentoring relationships in your ministry, you can help families mend relationships and become whole. It is important that youth workers always try to be advocates of family healing and wholeness.

Being in youth ministry for twenty-plus years *should* give me an upper hand on making bets as to which students will emerge in life as godly leaders and which will disappear into the shadows of spiritual apathy. Though sometimes I call it right, other times God surprises me. I have had many teens I mentored through rocky years of adolescence rise above it all to become strong, godly leaders in their communities and churches.

If you are a young youth worker, finish strong in your mentoring relationships. Don't give up. Remember that each person matures at a different rate and on different paths. Your strongest church leader tomorrow may be a diamond in the rough today. I call them late bloomers. You turn the soil, plant the seed, and water the ground, and then you wait. Some make you wait longer than others. And that is why we pray. God makes them grow.

> So neither the one who plants nor the one who waters
> is anything, but only God, who makes things grow.
> 1 Corinthians 3:7

Evaluation Questions:

1. Can you identify the fatal-flaw issues in your own life?

2. What do you think the most prevalent fatal flaws are in young people today?

3. How prepared do you feel you are to address these issues in the lives of your mentees?

4. How healthy would you say the relationships are between your teens and their parents?

Action Steps:

List out the teens or adults you are mentoring. Under each name, identify what you think may be their fatal flaws and areas for development. Next, assess how healthy you think their relationships are with their parents, siblings, peers, and other significant adults.

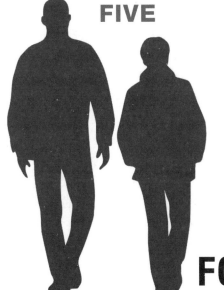

FIVE

FOUNDATIONS
FOR
MENTORING
RELATIONSHIPS

*It always protects, always trusts,
always hopes, always perseveres.*
1 Corinthians 13:7

I was ten years old when my dad asked me to join him on an evening service call. I was to be his assistant, installing a new lock on a customer's front door. The thought of spending time with my father thrilled me. And I was just as excited to be working alongside him and learning his trade. I watched his every moved as I handed him tools. Over the next few years, I went with him a number of times, and then he began to release me to work independently, carrying out tasks while he worked on other things. Eventually he sent me out to take care of calls all on my own.

My dad served as my first mentor. He mentored me in our growing father-son relationship by example. He mentored me by showing me how to do things like install a lock and cut a key. He also mentored me by releasing me to live and explore the family business on my own. As I gained his trust in my competence, he gave me more and more responsibility. I then began to duplicate his work and emulate his skills. Our relationship was founded in love, trust, and safety.

When the apostle Paul references his mentoring relationship with Timothy, he actually calls Timothy his son. Timothy has biological parents, but Paul treats him as his own son. Paul entrusts his life, his message, even his reputation to Timothy. Their relationship grows as they spend ministry time in their life-on-life mentoring relationship.

The Word became flesh and dwelt among us.
John 1:14

Jesus gives the perfect example of how to build a strong foundation for healthy mentoring relationships in his incarnation. In order to foster love, trust, and safety in his disciples, Jesus spends uncounted hours intersecting his life with theirs in daily routines, retreats, and teachable moments. Jesus's personal times with his disciples in and away from the crowds are critical to the foundation of his mentoring relationships and public ministry. Jesus does life with his disciples. Each time we observe Jesus doing ministry in the gospels, he is typically seen with some of his disciples by his side.

One of my mantras is to include someone else in life's tasks as often as possible in order to allow interaction and time spent in community. Significant mentoring costs personal time and necessitates reordering how you use your time. Your goal should be biblical *koinonia*. This Greek word is most often translated *fellowship*. It means to share or to partner, to invest in. As you invest your life in another, you cultivate *koinonia*. Reflecting back over many years of such investments in others, I am surprised by how much impact you can have on your apprentices through time, words, and actions. After several years of mentoring teens, I now observe some of my former students serving as pastors. The impact of simply providing a safe place for a mentoring relationship is immeasurable. But little can be much when we allow God to be in the center of our mentoring.

My wife and I have tried to practice this in our relationships with teens and also with our own children. This has translated into many hours of time spent with teens doing such mundane tasks as grocery shopping, cleaning, or installing a ceiling fan. My wife, Teresa, has had her mentees call to ask her what she is doing. Teresa, in the middle of trying to balance the busyness of raising three small children and keeping a house in order, often invited them to join her as she carried out her daily chores. Interestingly, many have been eager to take her up on the offer since they cherish interaction with her. They have come over and talked as they helped by holding a child or dusting an end table.

If you are married, it can be advantageous to allow those you are mentoring to see your relationship with your spouse in action. If you have kids, the time spent in your family's presence can provide a healthy model for the many teens who do not have healthy models in their own homes. In order for this to occur, you need to be sure to invest in the health of your family relationships. It is difficult to model what you do not already live.

Jared was a bright young athlete when I first came upon him in my new ministry. He grew up in a glass house as a pastor's kid. Everyone had unrealistic expectations of how he should act and behave. Like many PKs, Jared needed the space and ability to see himself through the lens of

45
∗

God instead of people. In some respects, Jared was a tough nut to crack, but I thought I understood his challenges. He came from a good home with great parents who loved him and tried to guide him straight. What he needed was a life-on-life mentor. So I gave him a little extra grace as we began our mentoring relationship.

We met weekly for a few years at a hole-in-the-wall diner and then at a Barnes and Noble, doing book studies and chatting about life with a small group of other high school guys. Jared came with me several times when I went to set up for an activity or to a speaking engagement. He also joined me on many of my extended speaking trips. Our time in the car and other places proved a fertile environment for growing a meaningful relationship. These times served to deepen the love, trust, and safety of our relationship.

To achieve love, trust, and safety in a mentoring relationship, you have to spend time. It's true that time is the one commodity that, once invested, can never be regained. But few investments are more worthwhile than a meaningful mentoring relationship. In order for a mentee to trust you and know that you are a safe person who has the mentee's best interest in mind, you will have to spend time together. There is no shortcut to building a healthy relationship. Depending on each person's history, upbringing, and temperament, the amount of time needed to create the right connection will vary.

Teens have frequently been hurt by the significant adults in their lives. Many develop jaded or cynical views that cause them to question motives and intentions of any adult who reaches out to them. In such cases, love is not easily accepted. Trust does not come quickly. Unfortunately, the human nature is naturally inclined to act selfishly. Even people's good deeds are often based on what they will get in return for their efforts. Divorce, abuse, rejection, and moral failure in leaders are just a few of the reasons for the growing skepticism of today's youth, necessitating a more extensive investment into your mentoring relationships. A loving relationship where trust exists and safety is felt does not come naturally or easily.

When Jared's mom developed cancer he, his brothers, and his parents needed the church to be their support. By the time this terrible trial came into Jared's life, we had been friends for several years. He had spent five years in my teen ministry and four years as an intern. I tried to continue to be available to Jared and his brothers as they lived through the hurt, confusion, pain, and eventual loss of his mom during his senior year of college. I watched from a distance as a godly woman I had long admired lost her battle to cancer. Many times I had no words for Jared. Some of the time, he talked about what was going on at home, and at other times our conversations centered on his schoolwork and internship. All I could do was be present.

As a mentor, it is important to remember you are not required to have all the right answers. In fact, mentoring is more about being present when the questions arise than it is about providing the solutions. When mentoring, you should avoid trying to make sense or assign meaning to your teens' trials and struggles. Instead, you should simply live life with them. God is the only one who can bring sense to it all. Trust can be broken when we attempt to give false hope or draw trivial meaning from life's encounters. Safety is best formed when you foster a place to share and then are present as you walk through life beside them. Your job is to point them to God for direction, by example.

Love, trust, and safety are fostered as we simply place ourselves in the intersections of our mentees' lives. And as life happens, God provides opportunities for love, trust, and safety to be created. Although being intentional is a key to developing a strong mentoring relationship, too much intentionality can seem inauthentic and contrived. Nothing serves mentoring better than time spent as life happens.

Today Jared serves as the founding pastor of a church named Liberti, which seeks to live, speak, and serve as the very presence of Christ for the neighborhoods of Center City and South Philadelphia. I did not expect my encounters with an eighth-grade boy to end up influencing the center of a city. But God can do great things as you faithfully give yourself to the life of mentoring.

47
*

Evaluation Questions:

1. What ways can you go about fostering love, trust, and safety in your mentoring relationships?

2. What challenges do your mentees have that make it difficult to create healthy relationships with love, trust, and safety as their foundational characteristics?

3. Can you recall a mentor who created this kind of an environment for you? How was it done?

4. What do you do on a regular basis that would allow for a mentee to be included your daily activities?

Action Steps:

Look at your schedule over the next three months. Identify a few opportunities to include your mentees in your life. Perhaps they could join you for a family activity. Consider your weekly routines as possible opportunities for spending time developing relationships with your mentees.

SIX

THE
IMPORTANCE
OF HONESTY AND
TRANSPARENCY

*A new command I give you: Love one another.
As I have loved you, so you must love one another.
By this everyone will know that you are
my disciples, if you love one another.*

John 13:34-35

When I first started in youth ministry, I was given the responsibility of shepherding a small group of teens in a church nestled in a rural college town. As I spent time with the guys in the group, it became apparent fairly quickly that I connected more easily with some than I did with others. It also did not take long to figure out that my attempt to develop relationships with a few of them was off base. A combination of their resistance to a new youth pastor and conflicting temperament dynamics made it difficult for me to engage them in meaningful friendships. At first, this was disappointing and an ego sapper. Pride and confidence were quickly replaced by humility and discouragement. How would I be a good youth pastor if some of the teens were not interested in relating to me?

Two things quickly became obvious. I was not going to reach every student personally. And I needed to enlist people who were different from me if I wanted every student to find an adult mentor in my ministry.

Discovering who you are and how you relate to others is instrumental in determining those you can most effectively mentor. And identifying the unique characteristics of others can go in tandem with this exercise. There are several characteristics, such as interests, background, and personality that bear impact on the dynamic. Here is a list of items I identified about myself:

High school football

Moderate viewing of sports on
   TV

Reader

Enjoy outdoors & hiking

Runner

Enjoy music

No interest in cars

Enjoy large gatherings

Attended public & Catholic
   schools

Nominal church family

Locksmith dad

New to church life

Outgoing

Struggle to understand nominal
   church teens

Interpersonal connections are more complex than a black-and-white list. Nonetheless, considering such things should help you determine the types of volunteers you may want to surround yourself with to ensure more teens have a natural adult mentor connection if it can't be you.

Your interests, background, and personality all play into whom you will most easily engage in a mentoring relationship. The opposite is also true. Those things that hold no interest for you can have equal influence. When guys start talking about the lineups for major league baseball teams, I start to space out. The extent of my interest in the sport is a casual viewing of the postseason, a couple of cigar boxes with my childhood baseball card collection, and a few years playing Little League. Differences do not mean you cannot or will not connect with someone. At the end of the day, love transcends, and can make differences seem trivial. If you take the time to express interest in young people and give attention to them, they will be willing to engage with you.

I called Ryan to see if I could drop by his family business after school. It was fall, and his family was harvesting the crops on their farm. I told him I would be interested in riding with him in the cab of his John Deere combine while hearing more about agriculture. He obliged. I spent that afternoon running back and forth down the rows of corn and learning about farming. On another occasion, he took me on a tour of their livestock, and I met his prize heifer. And on still another visit, we took the trek to his family's pig farm down the road. These were fun times for a city slicker. After the pig farm visit, I had to strip down and promise to take an immediate shower before my wife would let me enter the house.

On each visit, I asked Ryan questions about farming and his other interests. When some of his produce was entered into a farm show competition, I went to see his entries. I never knew there were so many types of squash and pumpkin. Despite our different backgrounds, I was able to connect with Ryan. But at the end of the day, one of my other male leaders was more effective in mentoring Ryan.

51
*

**Most of all, love each other as if your life depended on it.
Love makes up for practically anything.**
1 Peter 4:8, *The Message*

Jason and Rob were in the eighth grade when I started spending time with them. Their dads were both contractors, so their backgrounds and interests overlapped. Rob's interest in football and Jason's interest in music gave us other points of contact. I spent a few years meeting one on one with the pair and getting to know them better. I often visited their worksites. In fact, as a part-time youth pastor, I worked with them and their dads on occasion to make financial ends meet. Knowing their strengths, I was able to organize a few service projects during which they helped lead groups of their peers to build houses. This deepened our common bond, forming more significant mentoring relationships.

It is important that you don't try to be what you are not. Your expressions of interest in a teen's hobbies and extracurricular activities will seem inauthentic if one day you hate the ski slopes and the next you spend $600 on snowboard equipment to join your boarder teens. Being a poser and conforming to fit in will be a serious turn off to the average teenager. They can smell a phony right away. At the slightest hint of it, my teens yell, "Awkward!"

Teens need mentors who are self-aware and comfortable with who God made them to be. They don't want adults who try too hard to fit in. Being you is your best first step in becoming a mentor. This does not mean you cannot pick up a new hobby while getting to know your teens. You just need to have a genuine interest in the hobby. If you are cool, then you are cool. If you are not, then don't try to be. The adolescent years are tumultuous enough as they try to discover their own identities. The last thing they need is adults in their lives trying to do the same thing in the same juvenile ways.

Now in his forties, Mark is the essence of cool. Skateboarder, snowboarder, and surfer extraordinaire! He doesn't have to pose or act cool; he exudes it when he enters a room. But a short conversation with Mark lets you know that he has always loved extreme sports and the outdoors. Mark is one of those guys who works in order to play. His passions are sports and investing his life in others. He connects well with our extreme-sport guys, many of whom are in his small group. He knows the lingo better than they do. Mark knows who he is, and his teen guys see that.

Similarly, Eric has been working with teens for about six years. As an engineer and inventor, his technical savvy is impeccable. His brilliance tips the scales. If my computer freezes, I plead for Eric to come to the rescue. Each night he comes to the youth ministry, he intentionally makes his rounds and connects with his guys. Faithful, caring, and engaged, Eric has an ongoing impact in several teenagers' lives by shooting hoops and shooting the breeze. Eric is cool in his own right, but I have never seen him skating or surfing. Like Mark, Eric knows who God made him to be, and that makes teens comfortable around him.

Surrounding yourself with people who have hearts for youth mentoring and different backgrounds, interests, and temperaments can only strengthen your ministry's impact. Your team should be as diverse as the schools in your church's reach. It takes all types to mentor teens. Strong mentors must know who they are and learn the delicate balance of healthy transparency and honesty with discretion and wisdom. Teens need to see real people with real challenges and struggles. But adult leaders must learn the wisdom of discretionary sharing. There are some things shared that can be inappropriate and even potentially harmful to a mentorship's integrity. A good rule of thumb is to share only things from your life that you would also discuss with the mentee's parents present. If you are married, you should not hang out all your dirty laundry and embarrass your spouse or children.

I consulted with a youth pastor at a city church a few years ago. He told me about a mistake he made in not setting proper filters on the kind of information he thought was fitting for his mentoring encounters with teens. In an attempt to be relevant, he divulged information about his sexual relationship with his wife in mixed company. Instead of deepening his relationships, he made several teenagers feel very awkward. Knowing what is TMI is important. If you lack the ability to discern what is appropriate to share, ask another youth mentor for help.

Similarly, honest and appropriate sharing about your struggles and weaknesses can be helpful to your mentee's spiritual formation. I went into a midweek youth ministry gathering one evening after a challenging day. I had a difficult time focusing as I prepared to begin teaching. As I opened the Bible to teach, I first shared honestly about how I was feeling and the extent of my bad day. Then I told them that I appreciated their prayers and went on with my message.

The next morning, I received a call from Jacquelyn. She was the mother of a sophomore who had just started attending the ministry. She thanked me for my talk the night before and proceeded to tell me the incredible impact it had on her son. I asked her what specifically in my message had spoken to her son. She answered, "When you said you had a bad day, you gave my son hope. Sharing that you have struggles just like him made him feel like there was more hope for him and that he was normal. It inspired him to press further into his walk with Christ." I was dumbfounded and encouraged. I was also humbled that the words that made the most difference that night were not the ones I spent hours preparing but the few I shared in a moment of honesty and transparency from the heart.

Evaluation Questions:

1. What are your interests and hobbies?

2. What is unique about your background and upbringing? How might it influence your relationships?

3. What kinds of teens do you find it easiest to connect with, and what types pose you more difficulty? Is your youth ministry a balanced reflection of the schools in your area? Does your volunteer team reflect the same balance?

4. Do you find it easy or difficult to share your weaknesses with others?

Action Steps:

Look at your youth ministry and the interests, backgrounds, and personalities represented. Next, look at your congregation and make a list of people who might be a natural mentor to some of your teens.

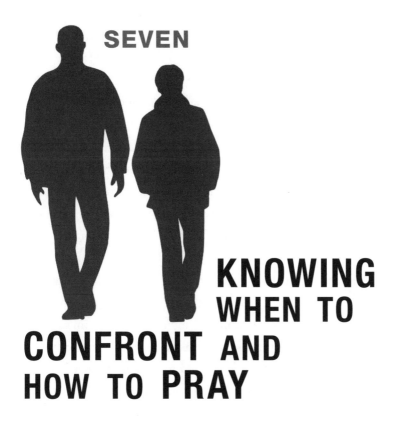

SEVEN

KNOWING WHEN TO CONFRONT AND HOW TO PRAY

Preach the word; be prepared in season and
out of season; correct, rebuke and encourage—
with great patience and careful instruction.
2 Timothy 4:2

John was in a mentoring relationship with me through his high school years and beyond. He was one of the more spiritually sensitive young people I had in the ministry. He served Christ through his godly lifestyle and inspired his peers to do the same. He brought friends from school to the youth ministry on a regular basis. When graduation came, John did not follow the path of his peers and flee small-town life for a distant college. Instead, he decided, like his brother, to work for the family business and stay in the area. This gave him the opportunity to continue his involvement as a young leader with the middle school teens.

John came to me in the spring of his second year of volunteering with the youth ministry and asked to talk. He told me he wanted to date a senior in the youth ministry. We had a frank talk. For obvious reasons, it was our policy that adult leaders could not date teens in the ministry. We had a lot of combined activities between the middle and high school ministries, so Sarah was frequently present when John was working with the middle school teens.

I let John know that he had a choice. Either he could date Sarah, or he could work in the youth ministry, but both could not happen while Sarah was still in high school. I expressed my concern for him and my feeling that he was not making a good decision for his future or hers. I suggested that they wait until she graduated to explore dating. It was a difficult decision for John to make since he felt called to ministry. But he was not interested in my suggested path. I communicated my disappointment in his decision as well as my continued love for him as we parted ways. His involvement in the ministry and our mentoring relationship appeared to be ending.

Within a few days of our conversation, John's parents asked to meet with me. It was evident in our time together that we did not see eye to eye. They left the meeting dissatisfied with my unbending adherence to our policy. I was perplexed that someone could not understand our values and our intent to protect both the teens and leaders. Since John's parents served as some of my strongest supporters and helped me fight many of our uphill ministry battles in the early years of the ministry, this was a particularly difficult time. They were my parents away from home. And now I was at odds with them.

Oftentimes, mentoring and ministry call for tough conversations. Few people enjoy conflict and confrontation. But to work with teens and their parents, you need to be able to share the truth in love. In the case of John, I had a few responsibilities in the balance: my commitment to the ministry, the protection of our teens and our safe ministry environment, and my commitment to John's welfare as his long-time mentor.

A few months after John made his decision, he came back to me and apologized. He told me that I was right and that he'd made a mistake in judgment. He said the relationship with Sarah was not healthy and that it ended abruptly. Unfortunately, it cost him respect from some of our teens and parents, and his place in our ministry. Confronting in love is not easy. But this is the tough work of life-on-life mentoring. If I had not been honest with John and adhered to our policies, I would have failed him as a mentor. But by confronting in love, God opened the doors for a continued relationship of respect with John.

Jenny grew up in an unstable home. Her mom divorced her dad when she was a few years old and married a military serviceman. The next few years of her life consisted of moving from one place to another, all over the country. She had very little relationship with her father or stepfather along the way. Stability was not a word that could be used to describe her family situation.

When Jenny entered adolescence, she moved to our town and began attending the youth ministry. Despite her rebellious appearance, Jenny truly wanted adults to invest in her life. My wife and Jenny entered into an in-depth mentoring relationship during the first year of Jenny's involvement in the ministry. Unfortunately, Jenny's behavior and decisions were often self-destructive. The task facing my wife was challenging as she peeled through the layers of hurt. Because Jenny did not deal with her hurt properly, she found herself in unhealthy relationships, time after time. She longed for the love of a father but sought it in the arms of guys who took advantage of her. Teresa regularly had candid talks with Jenny, trying to help her see that she needed to find her significance in

Christ and not guys. Jenny showed a desire to change, but her past was difficult to overcome.

When Jenny got pregnant, she moved into her own apartment and shortly thereafter gave birth to a little boy. Her life understandably became more complicated. Teresa's mentoring had to focus now on parenting skills, as well as trying to help Jenny move away from jumping into more unhealthy dating relationships.

Teresa remained a mentor to Jenny as long as she sought help and counsel and demonstrated a teachable spirit. For a few years, she took two steps forward and one step back. Through Teresa's tough grace and practical mentoring, Jenny was able to make it through some difficult years and poor decisions. On numerous evenings, Teresa met with Jenny and talked to her about the consequences of her actions, and she stood by her side when Jenny had to pay the piper.

Mentoring sometimes requires you to confront poor decision-making, fatal flaws, or sin in a mentee's life. This confrontation will likely not be a one-time event. It often takes ongoing coaching, with ups and downs along the way. Changing human behavior and character takes the Holy Spirit. In order to do this properly, you need to find a balance between truth and grace. You also need to know how to pray for your mentee and with your mentee. And you must constantly point the mentee to the need for a Savior who can guide us through the changes that need to be made in our lives.

Healthy confrontation in mentoring does not come naturally to most of us. When confronting a mentee, you need to make sure your words are constructive and not destructive. Constructive words point a person toward a reachable solution and address behavior and any character issues. They do not attack personhood. In other words, you need to provide a clear behavioral path for your mentee to take in order to overcome the issues you are addressing through mentoring.

For example, say your teen Phil has a difficult time fitting in with his peers, mainly due to his tendency to brag about himself and put others down. He does this in an attempt to make himself feel superior, but the result is that teens in the ministry avoid him at all costs. They find him obnoxious and his words hurtful.

There are two possible paths you could take in your mentoring response. You could go to Phil and tell him he is lousy at interacting with his peers and that no one wants to be his friend because of the way he acts. Although this criticism could serve as a wakeup call, it fails to give him a clear path for positive change. This response may be more destructive than helpful in Phil's spiritual formation.

Another approach could be to encourage Phil to stop trying so hard to fit in by making derogatory remarks about others in the ministry. You could explain to him that his tactics for fitting in cause people to avoid him rather than befriend him. Additionally, you could help him with some practical ways to express affirmation to others instead of making negative comments. And then pray for the Spirit to help him with the changes he needs to make. This would be constructive mentoring since it gives him a clear behavior to change to help solve his relational problem. Taking additional time to help address the root issue for Phil's poor relationship tactics could help him identify the underlying reason he self-destructs his friendships. And this would help him go beyond simply changing his behavior to changing his heart.

When the occasion arises to confront poor decisions, fatal flaws, or sins in a mentee's life, be careful to balance your truth and grace. You do this by aiming to be constructive. Timing and location are keys to confronting someone. As is the case when addressing any sensitive matter, try to confront privately, and when your mentee is not tired or emotionally drained. You should also make sure you are praying for the mentee and asking God to help you discern what to address and what not to address. Remember, mentoring is based on trust and love. If you have not established a healthy relationship, it will be more difficult to confront a person. At times, you will see behaviors in a mentee's life that concern you but you know it is not the right time to confront. In these moments, you should rely on the prayers you lift up on your mentee's behalf.

Jesus provides us with an example of how mentors can pray for their apprentices. In John 17, Jesus prays for his disciples with some specific requests. These requests can give you an outline of how to pray for your mentees.

- For God to protect them from the enemy (vv. 15-16)
- For God to make them holy through his Word (vv. 17-19)
- That they recognize God's glory in their lives and around them (vv. 4, 24)
- That they be in unity with each other and him so the world knows Jesus was sent from the Father (vv. 20-23)

In addition to praying for your mentees, it is important that you pray for God to give you discernment and wisdom as you speak into their lives. God has to be at the center of your mentoring relationships because every step a person takes spiritually is a work of God. Prayer is raised in this chapter because your need for prayer is never more critical in your mentoring relationships than when you are confronting someone with critical life issues.

Dan was a successful businessman I knew well because his children were active in the ministry. For all practical purposes, he was living the dream life: three children, a loving wife, a high-paying job, and a $2 million home on a few acres of prime land. As a new Christian, he was at the top of his game. But what looked in order on the surface was a brewing disaster just below the waterline. As I prayed and assessed the situation, it became obvious that a large part of the problem was Dan's ambitious work schedule. He traveled all over the country and left his family for weeks at a time. Even when he was in town, he was still in high demand by businesses within driving distance. They pulled him away from his family most nights of the week.

Dan and I had been meeting for a few months. I met with him one afternoon to express my concern, particularly for his oldest daughter. I prayed and explained what I thought needed to be the primary topic of our discussion. I suggested that his oldest daughter was at a critical moment in her life. I knew Dan was a person who liked to cut to the chase, so I tried to be direct yet constructive.

I told him, "Dan, you're a good dad, but I am concerned for Jill. She shows all the signs of a teen crying out for attention. You give her everything she needs in terms of material possessions, but right now what she needs more than anything is time with you. Honestly, if you don't make some changes in your work schedule and get more involved in Jill's life, I believe she is headed for a train wreck."

Dan appreciated my directness and the fact that I cared enough to confront him. I suggested ways he could spend time with his daughter while maintaining a healthy pace in his work.

Dan made some changes in his immediate schedule, but these changes did not last for long. Within six months of our conversation, his straight-A honors student was involved in a serious drug problem and repeated trouble with the police. Dan and I met a few more times to pray in the midst of the turmoil to help his family become stable again. The next couple of years were rocky for Dan and his family. He and his girls were the center of many of my prayers. I lost contact with him, but I did hear that Jill eventually turned things around and that God protected her and healed her strained relationship with her father.

Evaluation Questions:

1. How easy is it for you to confront others with their sin or fatal flaws?

2. How responsive are you to being confronted by others?

3. Do you have items you should be confronting in your mentees' lives right now?

4. How often do you pray for your mentees?

 Action Steps:

Read John 17:1-24 and study the way Jesus prayed for his disciples. Put Jesus's prayer for them in your own words and determine how you can pray for your mentees.

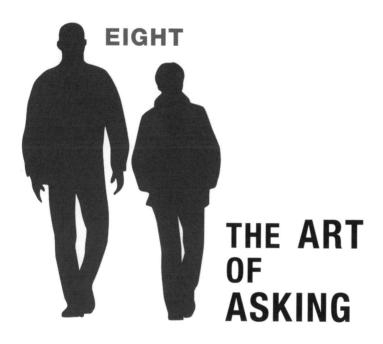

EIGHT

THE ART OF ASKING

Iron sharpens iron, so one man sharpens another.

Proverbs 27:17

I was in my first year of youth ministry when I met Don. He was my seminar instructor at a conference I attended in Chicago. The seminar was about developing a vision and strategic plan for youth ministry. Fresh into ministry and newly married, I had a lot of questions about ministry and how to maintain balance and margins in my busy life.

Don taught me a lot in that week. He had each of the young leaders in his class write a vision plan that we sent to him within a week of our return home. Because he lived relatively close to me, I sought out his time when we returned to our Pennsylvania ministries. Don was more than willing to give me time, despite having two teenage daughters and a growing youth ministry. Over the course of the next few years, I met with Don regularly and sought his counsel on many ministry and family matters. He was a Godsend and exactly what I needed at that point in my life. His humble demeanor, warm personality, and engaging interpersonal skills made me comfortable opening up and sharing with him.

Don was a good listener. He asked many good questions. He affirmed me when I headed in the right direction and shared practical advice when he thought I needed more coaching. When we met, he often spoke from his personal experience. He was obviously seasoned and had a lot to offer a young disciple like myself.

Don knew how to pull the best out of me and spur me to excel in my ministry strategy. He was not a hand holder but instead made me work and wrestle through ministry with the Spirit of God. Don's frequent references to his spiritual formation journey spurred me to engage with God at a deeper level through the spiritual disciplines.

I learned a lot about mentoring from Don over the years. One of the most significant skills he modeled for me is the art of asking questions. He knew how to pull things out of me and help me be more engaged in my own journey with Christ, rather than overtly directing my path. If you want to be a good mentor, you need to learn how to ask good questions. Good questions can cause mentees to dig deeper into their thoughts and hearts, ultimately finding God's direction. They point your mentee toward prayer and the counsel of the Word of God. But, if you are like most youth workers, you lean toward spending more time telling and giving advice than you do asking questions and listening. To be an effective mentor, you need to learn how to balance giving advice and telling against asking and listening.

You should spend about 75 percent of your time with mentees letting them answer your questions. Thus, you will nudge your mentees to be the ones making discoveries and arriving at decisions, rather than feeling they are being directed by you, step by step. It is important that you make the mentee do the bulk of the work with the help of the Spirit. If your mentees do not wrestle through their decisions, they will have more difficulty owning and implementing what they have learned. By encouraging the mentees to dominate the conversations, you help them to listen to themselves speak, vocally process new knowledge and ideas, and arrive at their own decisions for action with greater conviction.

Mentoring by asking questions and listening to the responses can serve a number of other benefits in your mentoring relationship. Using conversation in mentoring can prompt your mentees to be more prayerful as they struggle to discern God's voice in the process. And doing so can also help mentees learn how to listen to their own souls and prayerfully develop critical decision-making skills.

Have you ever mentored someone who struggled to make decisions and constantly asked you what you thought they should do in different circumstances? Paul was one of my interns a few years into ministry. He had strong relationship skills and an enthusiastic heart for pointing teens toward Christ. But he was afraid to make decisions. If Paul had his way, our mentoring relationship would have consisted of me giving him his agenda for the week and telling him God's will for his life.

When Paul asked me for advice, I responded with a question. This drove him crazy, but I knew he needed to develop the ability to seek God's will when making his daily decisions. He needed to gain a better understanding of who God had designed him to be as his servant. He also needed to develop as much confidence that God was leading him as he had that God was leading me. By asking questions and encouraging Paul to take steps of faith with his ideas and thoughts and praising him for his good judgment, I was able to help him grow in his confidence in God's work in his life. He began to make better and more confident decisions without consulting me all the time. And, over time, I gave him more responsibility. As a result, he became an exponentially better leader.

Good mentors keep mentees from becoming too dependent on them. Your goal is to help your mentees wrestle through personal decisions and draw their own conclusions. Sharing your stories and experiences and giving practical tips and advice can be helpful if they allow room for the mentees to discern how they should respond rather than direct their next steps. As such, your stories should inspire mentees to seek Christ, as well as to spur them to wrestle to arrive at their own Spirit-led decisions. A good mentor should be slow to give advice not because you lack the right answer but because you want to guide them to arrive at the right decision by asking questions. This method also helps your mentees develop a skill that can outlast your mentoring relationship. When you are no longer available to them, they will still have the ability to make Spirit-led decisions.

Listening is not enough to effectively incorporate this method into your mentoring relationship. You also need to ask good questions that help probe for deeper understanding and break past any sticking points or barriers that may exist. Failing to ask probing questions could leave your mentees locked in their present understandings of reality. But surgical questions can take them into new rooms they might not have previously explored. Asking good questions is a skill that takes practice. Building or including multiple questions on one line of thought can help probe deeper into a specific area. You should avoid asking too many questions that can be answered with one word or a phrase. Ask *what, how,* and *why* questions more than *who, when,* and *where* questions. For example, ask, "How did your parents' divorce impact you?" or, "What changed when your parents got divorced?" This leads to the possibility of more significant and in-depth conversation.

Adam was an interesting character. He was outspoken in his opinions, passionate about making his point, and seemingly angry at the world. He was also quick to speak critically and judgmentally against the obvious hypocrisy in other people's lives. Grace was not a fruit of the Spirit evident in his conversation. He was good at identifying the specks in other people's eyes. Interestingly, Adam was estranged from his dad and often complained about how his father was opinionated and critical and judgmental of others. Adam was deeply wounded by his dad's tough-love approach to parenting and, as a result, had next to no ability to relate to him. He ended up moving out of his family home at the end of his senior year and getting his own apartment.

Adam asked me to meet about once a month for advice and help over a game of air hockey or ping-pong. After only a few minutes of listening to Adam during our first visit, it was clear he was unknowingly becoming the father he despised. I asked him if he thought he was like his dad in any way. I also asked Adam to help me understand the difference between how he spoke so critically about people and the same trait in the father he hated so much. Through gentle yet precise questions and answers, Adam began to see his dad in the mirror. The very things about his father that turned him off were dominant characteristics of Adam's life. When this finally dawned on Adam, he was sobered and speechless. Over the course of the next several months, Adam intentionally tried not to be as critical and judgmental of others.

Adam still needs to work at forgiving his dad, but he has begun to stop reflecting the practices that caused him so much pain growing up. Asking questions and listening to responses fostered a teachable spirit in someone who might otherwise have been resistant.

Taking 75 percent of your time to ask questions and 25 percent of your time to give answers is a general mentoring guideline. Without doubt, you will be consulted as the expert on a specific subject during a mentorship. Someone will come to you and ask you for help growing in a certain skill or practice. At these times, the asking versus telling practice may not be as relevant. For instance, if you were training a person to disarm a bomb, you would probably need to spend more time instructing than asking what they thought they should do. Asking more questions in these circumstances, instead of giving instruction, would be cause for a panic attack. When your mentoring takes on a coaching component in an area where you are expert and the mentor wants to develop, your focus will obviously be more instruction based. However, even in these circumstances, the asking versus telling practice can be helpful once they gain more knowledge and understanding in their newfound skill.

Robbie was a high school senior who wanted to learn how to teach his peers at our midweek youth gathering. In our initial mentoring meeting, I coached him on how to develop his first talk and how to deliver it in an engaging manner. After Robbie's teaching, we debriefed his experience. I asked him several questions, including the following:

- What did you learn?
- What do you want to do differently next time?
- What do you want to do the same?

I also gave him some additional constructive criticism to help him improve his next talk. My tips addressed his body language, eye contact, and a few other items I knew would be simple improvements for him as he prepared to teach a second time. I spent a good deal more time talking than listening in our encounters, but I still used the asking versus telling principle to coach and teach Robbie to become a good communicator.

Evaluation Questions:

1. How good are you at listening? Ask the person you consider your best friend to help you evaluate your listening skills.

2. What portion of your mentoring time do you spend talking, and what portion is your mentee talking?

3. What other benefits do you see to having your mentee do more of the talking than you?

Action Steps:

Practice your listening skills with another youth worker in your ministry. Have them share their favorite childhood memory with you in two to three minutes. After they are done sharing, tell them what they just shared with you. Finally, ask them to tell you how well you did at the exercise in terms of accuracy and amount of content recited.

71
*

TYING
THE MENTEE
TO GOD'S STORY

And beginning with Moses and all the Prophets,
he explained to them what was said in all the
Scriptures concerning himself.
Luke 24:27

I grew up in what could be called a nominally churched family. Belief in God was a given in our home, but my parents rarely went to church. I have early childhood memories of my great aunt, with whom we lived, having me say my bedtime prayers. My mom sent my sister and me to mass on Sunday mornings, and I spent four years at a Catholic prep school. God came up in conversation frequently in our home, but he did not have a dominant role in our daily lives. Between brief conversations, parochial schooling, and the occasional viewing of an epic Bible movie on television, Jesus, faith, and the Bible played a minor part in my life and thoughts.

For all practical purposes, even after my parochial school education, I was practically Bible illiterate. I had little understanding of the Bible and God's restoration story. I had a familiarity with some of the popular Bible stories, but I did not understand how it all tied together, or its relevance to my daily life. It wasn't until my junior year of high school, when I gave my life to Christ, that I started to delve into the Bible's narrative. That's when I found the big picture of God's story and how I fit into it.

I am not sure I can find the proper words to describe the condition of the average young person's biblical aptitude today. It is not uncommon for a teen to ask me if Jesus is in the Old or New Testament, or who Moses, Paul, or Judas were. If you work with teens, you've probably had a similar experience.

Miah grew up in a Catholic home akin to mine. He started attending the youth ministry upon the invitation of a friend and became a part of my small group. Spiritually sensitive and with similar interests, we hit it off quickly. It did not take long for me to realize that Miah had little knowledge of God's story as revealed in the Bible, let alone knowledge of his part in God's mission. Many of our times together consisted of me fielding questions about the Bible and helping him wrestle through how it pertained to his life. Over the next several months, I met with Miah almost every week.

As a youth worker I try to help teens understand the broad themes and threads of Scripture's narrative by studying and observing it from Genesis to Revelation. This helps give our teens a healthy foundation on which to stand. Without this base, I would have had to spend a lot more time helping Miah learn the story of God. Instead, we were able to discuss what he was learning from the youth gatherings and how God's story should impact him and the way he lived his life.

When Miah first came into the ministry he was not an engaged follower of Christ. As he began to understand God's story and God's desire for him to be part of his mission, Miah decided to follow Christ, be baptized, and serve Christ. His discovery of the richness of God's restoration story helped him explore a relationship with God that included his being involved in the mission to restore man's relationship with God. Miah began to share God's love and story with his friends and also got involved in serving in the church.

As a mentor you need to help your mentees become centered in the story. Mentoring today's young people requires that you help them find their center in his story through the Bible. But to find themselves in it, teens need to know it. This is critical in our egocentric society. People need to be pulled back to the reality that the universe is much greater than them and that there is a God who is infinitely grander than all he has created. To gain true direction and meaning in life, everyone needs to understand God's restoration story: *Everything that exists finds its beginning and significance in him.* Trying to live your life without a foundational knowledge of God is like ripping a page out of a two-thousand-page NASA manual and trying to fly the next mission to the moon. You would be doomed to fail.

To live life without an understanding and centering in God's story is much the same. It is in understanding the narrative that teens can begin to understand God's redemption and desire for an active relationship with him. Some church teens may be familiar with the *dos* and *do nots* of Scripture but fail to learn about the heart of God. Having rules is not enough. They need to have a heart-to-heart connection with him.

A relationship requires connecting to the person of God. We best experience the person of God by reading, meditating, studying, and learning his story. Today's teens need a better grasp of more than just certain pockets of the Bible. They need to know more than the Ten Commandments and why they should wait until marriage to have sex. Your teens need to see God in action from Genesis to Revelation. Teens need your help connecting the dots between God's story and how they can live for and in him.

Josh was a Bible college graduate with a big heart for teens. He was well trained and gifted in building relationships and communicating with teens. When we taught through the Bible's narrative one year in the youth ministry, Josh came to me and said a light bulb went on for him. Although he grew up in the church as a pastor's kid and got a top-notch Bible school education, it was not until we studied through the Bible as a narrative that year that he really started to see the big picture, the common themes and threads. When Josh saw the plan of God unfolded in the Bible's pages, he had a deeper appreciation for God's mission and felt an even stronger, more personal tie to it all.

As a mentor, you need to help your mentees understand God's story and how they are part of the story. Everyone's story finds its beginning and end in his story. Effective mentors will work to help their mentees see themselves in and through the Scriptures by making sure they are engaging with the Word of God and growing in their grasp of the Scripture's narrative and its principles for life.

Being part of a church or youth ministry that is committed to helping young people be immersed in the Bible can help you be a more effective mentor. Due to the lack of biblical knowledge in today's teens, your work is more difficult than it was for spiritual mentors a generation ago. Consider it a positive challenge for most of your young people to be clean slates when it comes to biblical truths and God's story. This gives you a fresh start without as many preexisting misconceptions about God and the Bible.

Consider devising a plan to take your group of teens (whether it's your entire youth group, a small group you lead, or just your mentors) through the narrative of Scripture in a year. Once you do this, you can continue to help them see the context in the bigger picture through all your teachings. In my present ministry, we have walked through the metanarrative twice in seven years, both times over a period of about 38 weeks (a school year). We have also framed up the narrative in a shorter version on a summer missional equipping week and have included it in several devotional formats with simple images that fit on a bookmark. It can be read in five minutes.

We want our teens to be in engaged in and thinking about God's story. We want them to understand how it relates to their daily lives. In fact, instead of asking how it relates to their lives, we should challenge them to find their mission and purpose in God's story. Today's young people need to be challenged to come to grips with the reality that everyone needs to find their meaning and direction in him! The better your mentees grasp God's heart of love and redemptive plan throughout history, as revealed in the Bible, the more overwhelmed they will be by the reality that they are part of God's heart and plan. This will also help them further grasp the importance of being in biblical community and a mentoring relationship.

As their mentor, your teens will benefit from hearing you share your story and learning how you discovered the mission of God in your life. Bringing Scripture into your mentoring times and encouraging them to delve into the Bible is critical to a healthy mentoring relationship. When my wife mentors teen girls, she works with them to memorize scriptures that describe God's promises and his work in us. Writing God's Word on the heart of your mentees gives them something that can guide them throughout life, long after face-to-face influence is over.

How sweet are your words to my taste, sweeter than honey to my mouth! I gain understanding from your precepts; therefore I hate every wrong path. Your word is a lamp for my feet, a light on my path.
Psalm 119:103-105

Evaluation Questions:

1. How well do you understand God's story as revealed in the Scriptures? Could you explain it in five minutes to a mentee?

2. What personal goal would you set to gain a stronger grasp of God's story?

3. How well do you think your mentees understand the biblical narrative and the major themes and principles of Scripture?

4. How could you influence their knowledge and awareness of the biblical narrative?

5. How can you help your teens gain an awareness of their call to be a part of God's mission to bring the message of redemption to their peers and their world?

Action Steps:

1. Consider reading one of the following books that detail the story of God:

   • *The Mission of God: Unlocking the Bible's Grand Narrative,* Christopher J. H. Wright

   • *God's Big Picture: Tracing the Storyline of the Bible,* Vaughn Roberts

   • *A World Unbroken,* Barefoot Ministries

   • *A Walk Through the Bible,* Lesslie Newbigin (reprinted by Barefoot Ministries)

2. Review *A World Unbroken* by Barefoot Ministries as a possible tool to engage your teens through the narrative.

TEN

MENTORING THE WHOLE PERSON

That which was from the beginning, which we have
heard, which we have seen with our eyes, which we
have looked at and our hands have touched—
this we proclaim concerning the Word of life.
The life appeared; we have seen it and testify to it,
and we proclaim to you the eternal life,
which was with the Father and has appeared to us.
1 John 1:1-2

Laurie was a strong Christian teen living her life for Christ. She was engaged with God through his Word and prayer. Attending our youth ministry and church weekly, Laurie was someone who made everyone feel welcome. She brought energy to the room. She shared her faith in word and deed on campus, and she invited her friends to activities that were designed to help people connect to Christ. Laurie was part of our youth ministry teams that helped design and lead different aspects of the ministry. Everything about Laurie looked good to her friends, her mentor, and to me, her youth pastor.

But one afternoon Laurie came to my office after school seeking help. Over the next forty-five minutes, she openly told me about her struggle with her father. She said that until she turned fourteen, she had been close to him, but then something changed. She did not fully understand what was going on, but at almost sixteen, Laurie had spent almost two years in constant conflict with the man she admired and loved. The strain in her relationship with her father was beginning to become too much to bear. The impact of the conflict had begun to show in her countenance outside the home. She knew something needed to change, but she was not sure what.

That day, I gave Laurie a few assignments, and I prayed for her. Knowing her desire to honor God with her life, I explained that she had a responsibility to Christ to live and be Jesus to her dad. Regardless of his behavior, she was accountable for her side of the relationship. She needed to demonstrate love and respect for her father. I told her I wanted her to check back with me in one week.

We had check-ins for the next several weeks to see how things were going. Each time we met, I gave her another assignment. Her first assignment was to write her father five short notes on Post-its with words of praise, thanks, and love. She was to put them in places he would find them throughout the week, like his bathroom mirror, car steering wheel, or in his lunch bag. I told her to do this with no strings attached. In other words, she needed to make sure her dad knew she was not looking for something in return. She was not allowed to ask for the car keys or money for the night when or if he came and mentioned the notes. She was to simply express her appreciation for her dad.

At our next meeting, Laurie's homework was to ask her father if they could go out to breakfast for a date on a Saturday morning. She was to guide their conversation, seeking his advice concerning her future. Over the next few weeks, she shared how her relationship with her dad was beginning to display signs of a turnaround—less stress and little-to-no conflict. She also shared that she felt like he was making an intentional effort to deepen their relationship as well. I could tell Laurie was doing better for the first time in months. The steps she took honored Christ and helped rebuild the bridge with her dad.

Life-on-life mentoring requires you to really get to know the person you are mentoring. The more familiar you are with your mentees' spiritual health, family dynamics, school environments, aspirations, and relationships with their peers and the opposite sex, the greater the potential for growth and positive change. Laurie appeared to be doing well, but she needed mentoring in her relationship with her dad. Ignoring it only left her in an emotional and spiritual funk. God created us as whole people. You cannot expect ongoing spiritual transformation to occur in a person's life if some areas are left untouched or ignored. As a mentor, you need to help your mentees explore each area of their lives with the Holy Spirit's help.

Most people have the tendency to compartmentalize their relationships from God. They box God out of certain areas, whether purposely or unknowingly. Sometimes they do so because they are afraid of the need for change or out of fear for what God will ask them to give up. Other times they simply have blind spots.

As a mentor, your job is to help your mentees consider every area of their lives and challenge them to let God in. This takes prayerfulness on the part of both parties. A person's spiritual growth will only be as strong as that person's ability to master his or her greatest weakness, or areas of conflict, with the help of the Spirit. In addressing the whole person, you should consider three facets:

1. Spiritual walk; the spiritual practices that cultivate Christ's character

2. Missional lifestyle; level of engagement in living Christ's priorities and mission

3. Personal health; ability to maintain balance and margin

To assist your mentees with their spiritual walks, you need to help them consider how they best connect with God. Help them evaluate where they see the fruit of the Spirit represented in their lives. Prayer, time in the Bible, fellowship with other believers, and worship all impact a person's spiritual walk. And, although there may be similarities between the way two people approach God, he has uniquely designed each of us.

The way we approach God should freely reflect our differences. True, we all should pray and spend time in the Bible, but while one person may enjoy having personal times with God in a coffee shop, another may find that environment distracting. I find it helpful to journal my prayers and what I am learning in my time with God. It keeps me focused and disciplined. On the other hand, many of my friends find this practice tedious.

Helping your mentees develop their own ways to approach their spiritual walks is important. Giving them permission to do it differently from you is equally important. Teach them to change things up by trying new ways of connecting with God. It will keep their spiritual walks fresh and help them avoid legalism or the tendency to become dry in their approach. The goal of your mentees' spiritual walks is Christ's character being formed in them.

> **My dear children, for whom I am again in the**
> **pains of childbirth until Christ is formed in you . . .**
> Galatians 4:19

One litmus test for a healthy spiritual walk is to have them assess how they are reflecting the fruit of the Spirit in their relationships. In Galatians 5, these fruits are identified as being from the Spirit, which tells us that he is the one doing the work. This stands in contrast to legalism or a deeds mentality, which would simply come from a person's efforts to be a good person. In living the fruits of the Spirit, we reflect the character of Christ and not our own accomplishments.

> But the fruit of the Spirit is love, joy, peace, forbearance,
> kindness, goodness, faithfulness, gentleness and self-control.
> Against such things there is no law.
> Galatians 5:22, 23

Oftentimes, mentors are apprehensive about sounding legalistic by addressing the importance of practices like prayer and worship. The key is how you approach the subject. Spiritual practices—or disciplines— should be discussed as opportunities for growth in a person's relationship with God. These practices should be done more out of a desire to love God and know him, rather than obligation.

> It is for freedom that Christ set us free.
> Galatians 5:1a

As your mentees reflect the character of Christ in their spiritual walks, they should also be naturally taking on missional lifestyles that demonstrate their desire and commitment to live out Christ's priorities in his mission.

> We love because he first loved us.
> 1 John 4:19

A missional lifestyle is one that embraces and reflects God's heart for a world in need of his redemptive touch. It actively and intentionally goes out into the world, trying to share his love in word and deed. It is not just something one does during a particular time slot or ministry function. Instead, it is something you *are* in all your activities and interactions with people and God's creation. It is a different mindset than what some refer to as outreach. As a mentor, you need to help your mentees understand that missional living means they live as present-day incarnations of Christ.

Paul calls us Christ's ambassadors in 2 Corinthians 5, and we are called to make disciples of all nations in Matthew 28. Having a missional lifestyle is a new way of thinking that incorporates every moment of the day. It requires you to have your eyes wide open to the opportunities God gives you in every waking hour to extend his redemption to the world. Your goal is to help your mentees see themselves as missionaries to the world God has placed them in. Where they are, in each moment, is where God has them for his divine purpose of restoration. This means they will prayerfully pursue reflecting the character of Christ in all their interactions. Their purpose in life will be God's mission.

Unfortunately, experience has shown me that, all too often, young people who grow up in the church develop inclinations either to inoculate themselves from the world or to conform to the world and thereby, in both cases, fail to live out the mission of God. The challenge of the effective life-on-life mentor is twofold. Ask yourself, *Am I living the mission of God?* Then ask, *How will I help my mentees live the mission of God?*

As a mentor, you need to demonstrate this value in your life and then walk your mentees into the process of living it themselves. Your goal is to help your mentees understand what it means to join God in his mission of seeking and saving the lost. Our God is a missionary God, and as his people, we are called to join him in his mission. Helping your mentees understand how they can join God in his mission is fundamental to their spiritual maturity. Joining God in his mission is bigger than helping with a summer Vacation Bible School program or going on a youth mission trip to Haiti. Joining God in his mission means you live for him daily, trying to point everyone he allows to cross your path toward Jesus Christ. You do this through living love practically and by proclamation.

Casey came to Christ when Chris began to intentionally share Jesus with him. In my mentoring relationship with Chris, I tried to help him be more intentional in sharing his story and pointing his friends toward Christ. Chris had the desire, but he was nervous. However, as he stepped out through his faith in Christ and love for his friends, God honored and used his life to have an influence. Casey's transformation was the fruit of Chris's love and obedience.

When Casey began following Christ, he naturally lived the incarnation and told others about his relationship with God. Although his life was not perfect, people saw his love and the change in his life, and the change was contagious. Casey was not raised in the church, and, as a new Christian, he simply lived his life as a missionary. What was unnatural for Chris as a churched teen was natural for Casey as an unchurched new believer. As a mentor, your job is sometimes more difficult with the churched teens than with new believers who have not been immersed in church life.

Personal health is a hot subject in contemporary culture. Whether referencing physical, mental, or relational health, there is a plethora of resources that suggest ways to reach balance in one's well-being. Unfortunately, statistics seem to reveal the opposite phenomenon occurring in America's young people. Health in all areas of their lives seems to be getting worse instead of better. This is a time in our history when the need for life-on-life mentoring is more critical than ever. However, be careful not to overlook an equally great need: balance and margin in your own life. Today's young people are busier than any previous generation. Stress, anxiety disorders, and sleep deprivation are only a few of the symptoms that reflect the problem. We all need to be coached and challenged toward creating healthier margins in our lives for the sake of being healthier people and able to hear God's voice.

It is critical that you help your mentees evaluate their schedules, activities, and commitments and determine what needs to be altered. The role of parents and their pressure to over perform might also be an influence that needs to be addressed. To begin correcting the problem, you may need to provide coaching and education for the parents and families on a corporate level. Suburbs of major cities tend to have higher levels of unbalance and violation of the art of margin in people's lives.

Without margins, today's young people won't have the time or ears to hear from Jesus. Peace will be replaced with busyness. As a mentor, you want to help your apprentices learn to wrestle with the pressures life brings—pressures that have a tendency to actually suck the life out of us. Fullness can only be obtained as people allow God to transform them with his character and as they choose to join him in his mission and allow him to bring health and margin to their lives.

Evaluation Questions:

1. Which facet of mentoring the whole person comes naturally to you? Which is difficult?

2. Of the three facets referenced, which do you think your mentees most need you to address?

3. How do you think you can best assist your mentees in their spiritual walks?

4. Are you living out the mission of God in your daily life?

5. How can you help your mentees embrace God's mission and join him in extending his redemption to others?

6. Do you have difficulty keeping balance and margin in your personal life?

7. Is margin a prevalent problem in your mentees' lives?

8. What do you think is the best way to address the need for more margins in life?

 Action Steps:

Take time to evaluate individually with your mentees how they feel they are doing in the three facets of being whole people in Christ. Help them determine what areas they want to improve and the plan moving forward.

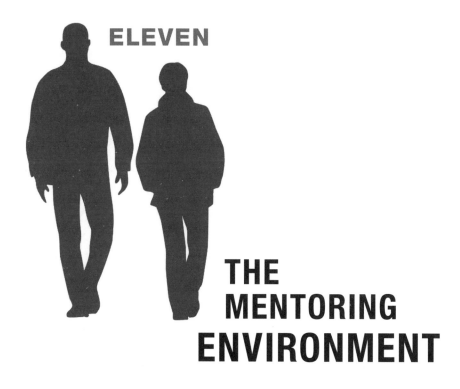

ELEVEN

THE MENTORING ENVIRONMENT

After this, Jesus and his disciples went out into the
Judean countryside, where he spent some time
with them, and baptized.

John 3:22

The spot was called Tumbling Run. It was my favorite hiking trail in South Central Pennsylvania and a great local site to take teens from my ministry for a few hours' getaway. A thick, wooded canvas of evergreens covered the rocky stream trail going up the side of a mountain, with several waterfalls cascading the smooth, stony cliffs at the top. It provided a challenging terrain and an awesome display of God's handiwork hidden just a few miles from town.

I had a small vanload of guys with me that day. It was a mixed crowd, including a few of my mentees and some of their friends. For the next couple of hours, we hiked, climbed, and waded. The trail gave a relaxing, distraction-free environment so we could get to know each other better and have significant conversations. While on the trails that day, God gave me the opportunity to build relationships and watch my guys be Christ to their non-Christian friends. When asked, I was able to share and help, but most of the day was simply having fun together.

I spent many afternoons on that trail with teens. Some of the time, it was with one mentee who wanted to talk and hang out. Other times, it was with a group of two or three who wanted to pray together and interact with the Bible at the top of the cliffs. Finding safe and conducive places to conduct your mentoring is important. A coffee shop, living room, or trail can provide the context needed for mentoring, depending on what you are trying to accomplish. The key is to know your goals and then pick the best environment to accomplish them. Essentially, mentoring can happen anywhere. The general principle is that it happens whenever you are with your mentee. However, the level of impact is influenced by how intentional you are in choosing the place and guiding your time and conversation. There are five varied environments you can use for mentoring:

1. a safe place
2. a common place
3. a retreat
4. on the run
5. in ministry

A safe place is a location that fosters confidentiality and provides privacy for your conversations. If you are discussing sensitive matters, then you probably need a place that is free of potential eavesdroppers. Or, if you need to meet one on one with a teen of the opposite sex, a safe place is the best recommendation. It may need to be in an office, the teen's home, or a room in your church that is not secluded but still provides some level of privacy. If you are mentoring someone of the opposite sex, your door always needs to be open to protect you, the teen, and your ministry from unnecessary accusations. In such cases, I sometimes meet on a park bench in front of our church office. This provides a suitably private and quiet place that is still visible to the public eye. I recommend not making a safe place the norm for your meetings, but it may be necessary for a season, or under certain circumstances, to respect the privacy of your mentees.

A common place is a comfortable environment that is relaxed and helps break down walls. For most of the years I have been in ministry, I've met with a few guys before school at a bagel shop or breakfast nook. At the crack of dawn, once a week, we meet to talk about life, pray together, read the Bible, and challenge each other in our spiritual walks, joining God in his mission. Early morning is an odd time for teens, but when you express interest in spending ongoing time with them—and include food in the offer—success is in the works. I often see mentor/mentee relationships being carried out in coffee shops. Coffee shop atmospheres are relaxed and inviting.

A mentoring retreat is a getaway time where you choose a place to take your mentees (either individually or in a group) for an extended period of time. The length of your stay can be anywhere from a few hours to a couple days. The general idea is to provide a change of scenery that will naturally prompt bonding and sharing. I like the outdoors for my retreats. If you are from a country setting, you may choose to retreat to a city. Any context can work that is conducive to an extended time for dialogue and relationship building. It is all about how you design the time.

If you have a family in your church with some sort of vacation property, you may want to consider asking if you could use it for overnight mentoring retreats. Plan your time in advance with different exercises that include prayer, sharing, creative worship, and Scripture. Depending on the maturity of your mentees, you could include them in the planning. You can vary your time between group mentoring and one-on-one activities.

On-the-run mentoring is when you include your mentees in your everyday activities. Demonstrate that you are a normal person by inviting them to join you in your routine activities. It also gives them a peek into your life.

As a single youth worker, Phil often had one or two of his teen mentees with him. He was someone who taught me how to do mentoring on the run well. It was not uncommon for Phil to take a few guys with him while running errands. His grocery shopping stories are my favorites. Phil made grocery shopping into a game. He split his list in half and had them race through the store to see who could get to the checkout line first. Though I wondered if he ever left the store with everything he intended, I loved the creativity of his method.

You can also do mentoring while involved in a ministry activity. Inviting a teen to come alongside you while you are doing ministry can be a great environment for modeling and building relationships. I had a speaking engagement that started at midnight on a college campus. I was supposed to be talking to eight hundred teens about sex and dating. It's an interesting topic to address at midnight on a college campus! Josh and Jared were two high school seniors I was mentoring at the time. They agreed to keep me company for the drive and assist me in my ministry that evening. Consequently, their presence at the event provided a great opportunity for conversation on the ride home.

One general rule in ministry is that you should never do it alone. Including your mentees in your ministry activities can be a healthy way to mentor and produce future leaders. In the past, I had a mentoring ministry program where we teamed a high school student with a ministry worker in church for a year or more. We had teens serve alongside their mentors in children's ministry, the tech team, as greeters, and in our café area. The impact was significant for the teens involved.

You can also intentionally design a mission trip as an aid in your ongoing mentoring relationships. Taking teens to different cultural contexts to serve will draw them out of their comfort zones, producing new experiences and teachable moments. The extended time you encounter on a mission trip inevitably gives you a deeper view into your mentees' lives. Living with someone for a week or more at a time can reveal interpersonal skills—or lack thereof. I suggest doing local missions and service with your mentees before considering overseas or even cross-country trips. In each case, training and team building should precede your trips.

Recently, I needed to teach at a school on the Black Sea for a week. I was also expected to work with a small church startup in a nearby village. Rather than making the trip alone, I took three young guys to keep me company and assist me in ministry. Traversing through six international cities, on five planes, and then ten hours in a compact car can teach you a lot about people. During our twelve days of ministry in Eastern Europe, we were able to have many conversations about our spiritual walks, joining God in his mission, and how well we were doing with balancing all the various aspects of our busy lives.

We read that "Jesus often withdrew" (Luke 5:16) from his normal activities. Regularly, his disciples join him. Jesus uses these occasions to mentor his disciples. Determining where you do your mentoring is important. Varying the environment will strengthen the mentoring bond in most relationships.

The key is to be intentional. No matter which environments work best for your mentoring relationships, it is critical that you create a sense of hope, expectation, reliability, and stability for your mentees. Hope and expectation mean that you help your mentees anticipate what God is going to do in them and through them as you challenge and encourage them forward in their development. Your desire is for teens to keep their eyes wide open for God's work. Teens need to be taught to expect God to keep his promises. They need to be taught to expect him to work in and through their lives in supernatural ways.

Many of today's young people have no one in their lives infusing them with hope. No one believes they can change and be difference makers. The job of the mentor is to help them see beyond where they are and look forward to where God wants to take them, and believe that it can actually happen.

Stability and reliability are equally important in the mentoring environment. Many of today's teens lack adults in their lives who provide true stability and reliability. Many have been let down by adults. In mentoring young people, you need to provide a consistent, stable, and reliable environment. Your mentees need to know you are trustworthy and responsible and that, if you say you are going to meet them, you will. These characteristics can build trust. Young people need to see God helping normal people live their lives with Christ's righteousness. This does not mean that you as a mentor need to be perfect. Instead, it means you strive to be a person worthy of your mentees following after you as you follow after Christ.

It is also necessary to determine how often you meet and the length of a typical mentoring session. This depends on what you are trying to accomplish, your availability, and the availability of your mentees. Each mentoring relationship is different and needs to be designed according to its specific goals. The logistics of my mentoring relationships are guided less by a system and more by principles and relationship values. I try to evaluate each relationship's investment and success on a regular basis. Adjustments can be made along the way.

While I have some regularity to my mentoring times, I also like to allow for extra times with my mentees that come up as life happens. However, some consistency is fundamental to success. Remember, the primary difference between life-on-life mentoring and other types of mentoring is the ongoing face time. You may meet once a week or once every other week. Some of the time, you may choose to gather with more than one mentee at a time, if it helps you accomplish dynamic goals like built-in peer accountability. Regardless, you will likely also need to include one-on-one mentoring times to meet some of the goals that are better accomplished in a more personalized approach. Each mentee needs personal face time with you that includes focused conversation, custom fit to individual needs.

Some life-on-life mentoring relationships will be focused and intense for a six-month period and then taper off. Others may last for a lifetime with continued check-ins. Ideally, your goal is to take a young person through adolescence and into adulthood. If you begin mentoring a teen in the ninth grade and then provide continued, regular connection times into the first year of college or work, you will have given that teen a strong, ongoing mentorship in those years of transition.

As the mentee moves into post-high school, periodically create some check-in points over holidays or breaks. When college students come home for Thanksgiving, Christmas, and spring break, invite them to join their previous high school mentors for a night of food and catching up with those from the ministry. The periodic checkpoints let graduates know there are still people who care about them and want to be in their corner. Even when the mentees have left the youth ministry, continue to check in. It provides the opportunity for ongoing impact and support in another challenging period of life.

Evaluation Questions:

1. Which ministry environment comes most naturally for you?

2. Which one is the most challenging for you?

3. Can you think of ways that you can mentor on the run in your present mentoring relationships?

4. Are there others in your church who may be able to provide mentoring opportunities by allowing teens to come alongside them in ministry for a season?

Action Steps:

Collect a list of the teens who serve and the places they now serve in your church. Ask the adults they serve alongside if they would be willing to consider being intentional at mentoring these teens. Design a thirty-minute mentor-equipping session that you can provide for these adults.

TWELVE

THE POSTURE OF THE MENTOR

Join together in following my example, brothers and sisters, and just as you have us as a model, keep your eyes on those who live as we do.

Philippians 3:17

Personal experience is one of life's best teachers. If you engage and pay attention, you can learn a lot. You can also learn a lot from watching and observing others. My years of mentoring and of being mentored have shaped both how I understand mentoring and how I approach it.

By observing my mentors and learning from my failures and successes, I have found that your posture in mentoring is critical. By posture, I mean the way you approach your mentoring relationship and the perception you create of yourself for your mentees. Your posture influences the level of success you will have in helping your mentees mature. I have found at least five foundational components to your posture. You must be:

- approachable
- humble and teachable
- Spirit led
- fully present
- dynamic in your own relationship with Christ

Approachable. In my first semester of college, I needed someone to talk to as a mentor. I was still a relatively new Christian, and I was away from home for the first time. I was physically separated from those who had been mentoring me the previous two years as a new Christian. I decided to approach the person who made the most sense to me in my new environment: my faculty advisor. One afternoon in the winter of my freshman year, we met in his office. We already knew each other pretty well, since he was one of my teachers, so I thought we would not have to waste much time with introductions. I enjoyed his classes and was learning a lot from him. Not too far into the conversation, he referred to me as Mark instead of Mike. He did this a few more times, even after I corrected him. In our time together, I felt a sort of professional distance in his demeanor. I was the student, and he was the professor. When our fifteen-minute meeting was up, I walked away feeling disappointed and like I had wasted fifteen minutes of both our time.

It is important that your mentees feel you are approachable. If you do not exude an approachable demeanor, they will have a hard time opening up and being transparent with you. Being approachable has a lot to do with being a warm and engaging person. Demonstrating your interest in your mentees by being friendly, personable, and intent on getting to know them as individuals will help. If you keep your times together sterile and create the feeling of a sage-to-pupil relationship, chances are, your mentees will have a difficult time connecting with you. This does not mean it is unhealthy for your mentees to look up to you or think of you as someone with great wisdom and insight for their lives. Part of the reason young people want to spend time with you probably has something to do with your being seasoned and more experienced in life than they are. But it is important that you help them see you as a person.

Probably without realizing it, my college professor made me feel as if he was not interested in me as a person. His failure to get my name right and be personable in our first one-on-one meeting together gave us a rocky start. Perhaps he was having a challenging day. Over the next few years, I found him to be more approachable and interested in me as a person. As a young person, I was nervous going into the office of a biblical scholar, someone I looked up to as a model. Your teens may have this perception of you as a leader. This kind of respect is healthy and good, but you also need to help them know they can approach you.

Jesus demonstrates the principle of being approachable in his posture through his incarnation and daily encounters with people.

And the Word became flesh and made his dwelling among us.
John 1:14

Despite his divinity, he lives as someone who is approachable to common people. He spends time with the religious and the sinners, the schooled and the unschooled. He walks with people, eats with people, laughs with people, and cries with people. He meets them in the daily intersections of their lives.

I was asked once to do a funeral for the grandfather of one of my students. I went to the family's home and spent some time listening to them and praying for them. I went to the viewing later that week. After the funeral, I spent a few hours interacting and getting to know the family better. As we sat over a meal talking about life, I moved from being a pastor to being a friend. The degree that you can make yourself approachable to your mentees will make a greater impact on their lives.

Humble and teachable. One of the things that impressed me the most about Don was his humility. He never bragged or made himself sound better than others. He often shared what he was learning and the things in life that were challenging him to grow as a person and as a Christian. His unassuming spirit and affirmation of my thoughts and ministry practices made me feel more relaxed when we met. I was fresh out of college, and he was a twenty-year ministry veteran. How, I thought, could he learn anything from me? But in our times together, he demonstrated that he did learn from me and that he wanted to continue to do so.

A few years into our mentoring relationship, Don asked me to collaborate with him on an international mission trip. We joined our summer teams and did ministry in the Netherlands together for three weeks. During the planning and actual ministry time, he treated me as an equal. He modeled for me what a servant of Christ and a good mentor should be like.

Your ability to reflect a posture of humility and a teachable spirit helps your mentees know you are a real person. It makes them feel valuable in the relationship and more comfortable sharing their thoughts, ideas, and questions. If you are a learner as well as the teacher, then it makes even more sense to your mentees that it is okay for them to be learners. Taking a posture of humility and a teachable spirit shows your mentees what they need to be for your relationship to be a success.

Mentoring is a relationship and, as such, needs to possess a two-way dimension. Reciprocity needs to exist. Nowhere is this posture more important than in a mentoring relationship between an adult and a teenager. In a culture that creates an inclination toward self-sufficiency and pride, teenagers need to have adult mentors who help them see that the opposite posture is more beneficial and helpful to them in their growth. Jesus models humility by constantly assuming the posture of a servant toward people who should be serving him.

For even the Son of Man did not come to be served, but to serve,
and to give his life as a ransom for many.

Mark 10:45

Spirit led. Glenn was my RA in college. He lived across the hall from me on the third floor of our dorm. He made it known to all the guys on the floor that he was available and at our disposal during reasonable hours. I often knocked on his door seeking advice or encouragement or sometimes just to talk. Glenn gave me a sense of his earnest desire to lead me toward Christ and God's plan for my life. His posture was one that demonstrated a desire to be Spirit led. As I shared my questions and struggles, Glenn always prayed for me and often pointed me to the Scriptures for wisdom and encouragement.

The posture of a healthy mentor is Spirit led. Your mentees should get the sense that you look to God for the discernment and wisdom you pass on to them. In the gospels, Jesus demonstrated a spirit of surrender to his Father. He did so through his prayer life and constant reference to Scriptures.

The Son can do nothing by himself; he can do only what he sees his
Father doing, because whatever the Father does the Son also does.

John 5:19

103
*

A healthy mentor's posture should be centered in prayer and Scripture so the mentees feel they are being directed by God. Being Spirit led in your mentoring relationships gives your mentees a connection to the eternal.

Fully present. Have you ever had the sense that the person you were talking to, face to face, was not listening? I had a professor in grad school who always seemed distracted. Frequently I sensed his lack of presence when I talked to him, primarily due to his failure to make eye contact. He had a habit of looking at other people in our vicinity instead of at me. As a result, I have a tendency now to put my back to what is going on around me and focus my attention on the person I am talking to so that person knows I am paying attention.

We live in an easily distracted society. It is not uncommon to be in a restaurant and observe two people sitting across from each other, both looking down at their phones as they text other people. In our culture, we have a difficult time focusing on the person right in front of us. Teens need mentors who can be fully present when they are meeting together. If you give the appearance of being busy or interested in other people when you are meeting with your mentees, you risk giving the impression that they are not important and that your time together is not valuable to you. I have been guilty of this phenomenon even with my own children.

My daughter gets frustrated when we are together if I constantly answer my cell phone. The rule of thumb should be that the conversation that is most important at present is the one with the person standing right in front of you. When you are meeting with mentees, it is important that you give them the sense that, in that moment, they are the most important people in the room with you. Being fully present in your mentoring posture is something that will likely take an intentional effort on your part. It is becoming a countercultural behavior, but one we need to recapture in all our relationships if we want them to be substantial and meaningful.

Dynamic in your own relationship to Christ. The first thing that attracted me to Joe as a mentor was his dynamic relationship with Christ. He had a fervor and intensity about him that came out in our first encounter at church. I was not a Christian at the time. But I did want to learn more about the Bible and what it meant to know Christ. Joe's excitement intrigued me. He made me more interested in faith just by being around him. When we met after church on Sunday afternoons at his home, he radiated an obvious desire to pursue Christ and grow in his relationship with him. As we opened the Bible together, Joe shared fresh insights he was learning about being an authentic Christian. He also shared the changes that were occurring in his life because of his faith.

I still remember one of my first afternoons with Joe at his family's home. We were talking about the poor. He showed me several passages in Scripture that convicted him and influenced his lifestyle of ministering to the poor. I saw a jar on his dresser filled with change. When I asked him about it, he told me that he saved all his change to give to a ministry that cared for the needs of those less fortunate. That evening, I went home and found a jar so I could start saving money for the poor, just like my new mentor.

Joe's dynamic faith set the course for my accepting Christ as my Savior later that year. He also provided me with a clear example of what it meant to live for and like Christ. Joe lived a dynamic faith that made me want to become an active part of God's people and mission.

Your mentees need a mentor who is engaged and active in the faith. They need your energy to motivate them toward the same kind of lifestyle. Young people today need models in their mentors who not only go to church and live upright lives but who also have a zeal and excitement that scream, *I am alive in Christ! He has changed me! And now I want to be a part of his mission!* A posture of dynamic faith influences the trajectory of your mentees' lives. This means you need to stay challenged in your pursuit of Christ and his kingdom. Your excitement (or lack of excitement) in your faith will have a powerful influence on your mentees.

Evaluation Questions:

1. Which component of a mentor's posture do you need to give the most attention to improving?

2. What else do you think is important for mentors to practice in their posture to be effective?

3. Who in your life has provided you with the best example of the proper posture of a mentor?

 Action Steps:

Take a few moments to evaluate yourself in light of the five components of a mentor's posture. Ask your mentees to help you evaluate your posture. Which component should you work on the most, and what steps could you take to improve?

THIRTEEN

CHOOSING
YOUR
MENTOR

*And the things you have heard me say in the
presence of many witnesses entrust to reliable people
who will also be qualified to teach others.*

2 Timothy 2:2

If you see the value of mentoring for others, then you understand the value of being mentored yourself. In addition to the benefits to your personal development, it leads by example to the teens you mentor.

As an adult, the shape of your mentoring relationships and how you engage in these relationships will take on a different form than the adult-to-teen mentoring relationships you foster. Unlike the mentoring relationships you have with teens, you, as the mentee, will probably need to be the one initiating your mentoring relationship. Potential mentors are not as likely to pursue you. You will also need to identify the path you want your mentor to explore with you.

Identifying the best person to mentor you is not an easy task. It takes prayer, thought, and determination. At times, God has placed people in my life who were obvious mentor candidates. At other times in the journey, it has been more challenging to find mentors and has required more effort on my part. In choosing a mentor, you should try to find someone who:

1. Is vibrant in his or her walk with Christ
2. Is older and wiser than you are
3. Is experienced and gifted in the areas you want to give special attention to
4. Believes in you and your potential
5. Can speak the truth to you in love
6. Is available to make the investment you need

If you want to grow in your walk with Christ and utilize a mentoring relationship to foster that growth, you will want to pursue a mentor who has an active, growing faith relationship with Christ. You should see your potential mentor as a person who reflects the character of Christ and the priorities Christ holds. Your mentor should be a good model and someone who spurs you to pursue Christ's character and his priorities through your life. The mentor's example should demonstrate to you this path and spur in you a desire to pursue it more.

During my first ministry, I had a few people from my church who invested in me on a regular basis. They were seasoned saints who motivated me to pursue all that God had for me. They had walked through a lot more life than I had and had a lot to teach me. Their passion for Christ and tenacious service of him in ministry attracted me to them. I wanted to be like them. So I pursued spending time with them in hopes their lives would rub off on mine.

Age most often comes with wisdom. But wisdom does not always come with age. In trying to choose your mentor, look around your church and identify those who have walked through more of life than you have and now demonstrate maturity in spirit as a result. You should choose someone seasoned by life's ups and downs. A good mentor has typically experienced some suffering. Suffering builds character and greater dependence on God.

> Not only so, but we also glory in our sufferings,
> because we know that suffering produces perseverance;
> perseverance, character; and character, hope.
> Romans 5:3

Suffering has a way of chipping the rough edges off of people if they allow God to grow them through it, rather than allowing their suffering to destroy them. By virtue of age, we experience more adversity, and more character is developed. A good mentor is going to have some age and wisdom that are beyond your own. I know I am a better mentor today than I was twenty years ago.

Knowing the areas you want your mentor to help you in will influence the type of person you choose as a mentor. You do not want a mentor who is in the middle of experiencing the same struggles you have. Nor do you want one who does not possess gifts where you want to grow. Pick someone you think can help you grow in the areas you desire.

Ed encouraged me to press on as he coached me and helped me with my teaching skills. He nudged me toward improving by expressing his confidence in my gift and by coaching me to become better. As a result of Ed's belief in me, I became more confident in pursuit of my gifting for Christ. Your choice in a mentor should be someone who believes in you and sees your potential and who can help you move toward your goals.

Like Ed, Chuck coached me to be a better teacher. Over several months, Chuck was a mentor for me in my teaching skills. He encouraged me and expressed belief in me and my gifting. But he also gave constructive criticism to help me improve and become a better teacher. It did not always feel good when Chuck and I talked, but it definitely spurred me toward refining and sharpening my gifting.

You need a coach who is not afraid to hurt your feelings by speaking the truth in love. You need someone who cares more about your development than about your comfort. Good mentors will help you mature by pointing out places you can grow and improve. They will be able to give you clear directions that help you take steps toward improvement. If they have not done a better job of mastering the areas where you want help, then they will not be able to help you grow. Mentors cannot take you somewhere they have not already gone.

Make sure the person you want as a mentor is available. Can you align your schedules so you have good times to meet together? Determine what you think you need in a mentoring relationship in terms of time and schedule, and be prepared to communicate that when you get together. You may need to be creative to find meeting times.

By identifying the characteristics you seek in a mentor, you will narrow your search for the best mentor. Pray, write out your plan and needs, and then determine when you will make your request of your mentor.

Before approaching a potential mentor, you should do a personal assessment and consider identifying the following:

1. Your hopes and expectations for the mentoring relationship
2. Any specific areas where you desire coaching
3. Any information you think a mentor needs to know about you up front
4. Your best means for learning and growing as a follower of Christ

Knowing what you hope for and your expectations will help the person you approach determine whether he or she can provide you with what you desire. If you don't paint a clear target, you should not expect a clear shot. Knowing your focus will help your mentor plot out a path and course of action.

In addition, you should be able to explain the specific areas you think your mentor will be able to help you with. Write out your goals for the relationship and then share them with your potential mentor. This will cultivate a conversation that should help you both know if it is wise to pursue a path together. It is also helpful to ask the potential mentor if he or she can identify other areas God may want to focus on for your development. If the mentor already knows you fairly well, he or she may recognize something about you that you have not identified. Mentors may be able to detect gift areas that can be drawn out or see some of your blind spots or fatal flaw areas that can be overcome. This should be a two-way conversation that is spurred by you initially sharing your goals.

Identifying these factors will also help you be prepared for when you approach your potential mentor. The more thought you give prior to your introduction and proposed mentorship, the more chance of securing the right mentor and beginning your mentoring relationship on the right foot.

Don't forget that it is always helpful to utilize the other types of mentoring relationships discussed in chapter 1. They can supplement the development your life-on-life mentoring provides. Circumstantial, indirect, and peer-to-peer mentoring are all beneficial and, at times, necessary for your development.

At present in my life, I can identify three circumstantial mentoring relationships, several indirect mentoring relationships that include a few authors I read regularly, and three peer-to-peer mentoring relationships. I have had life-on-life mentors move out of my life on a few occasions over the years. When transitions such as these happen, you can utilize the other types of mentors at a greater level.

I am not sure where I would be today if God had not given me my mentors. Having mentors who make a life-on-life investment in you will challenge you, grow you, and ground you. It will give you strength and encouragement when hard times come your way, and a sounding board and prayer partner when you need advice.

The Bible is full of good examples of leaders who seek to be mentored. When Moses oversees the nation of Israel, he needs mentoring in his leadership skills and ability to delegate and develop the leaders around him. He is mentored by his father-in-law, Jethro, in Exodus 18.

All mentors and youth workers need mentoring. The goal is for your mentor to take you places you cannot go on your own. Being mentored will also help you be a better mentor to your students. As you learn from being mentored, you will be able to sharpen your mentoring skills. Being mentored will give you a glimpse into the vantage point of those you are mentoring. It will help you see through their eyes and understand how you can communicate better with them and help them grow. Being mentored is important for your spiritual walk and the walk of those you lead.

Evaluation Questions:

1. In what areas do you need to be mentored the most right now?

2. Who in your life is a possible mentor candidate?

3. How could you approach a potential mentor?

Action Steps:

Find a time and place you can focus to write out your thoughts, expectations, hopes, and goals. Additionally, take time to pray. Have paper, pen, and Bible on hand for this exercise. Review this chapter and follow the instructions it gives you to prepare for your mentorship request. Form a one- to two-page document that you can present when you get together with your prospective mentor.

113
*

FOURTEEN

LESSONS FROM EXPERIENCE

Listen to my instruction and be wise;
do not disregard it.
Proverbs 8:33

I have earned a few degrees in my last twenty-five years of ministry. They may not be from the most prestigious schools, but they are definitely from the most practical and transformational ones. With the proper coaching, much of what I learned can actually transfer to another youth worker with a teachable spirit. One of the best schools I attended is not accredited, but it gives valuable classes that are transferable and not easily forgotten.

I am referring, of course, to the school of hard knocks. I have learned many valuable lessons from my personal mistakes and from the mistakes of those around me. Twelve lessons that should to be applied to your mentoring ministry are as follows:

1. Don't forget the parents and families of your mentees.
2. Be prayerful and selective in those whom you invest your life.
3. Make a plan.
4. Be flexible.
5. Expect some disappointments.
6. Beware of deceit.
7. Don't lose hope.
8. Call others to join you.
9. Take time to evaluate.
10. Don't try to change your mentees.
11. Keep growing.
12. Know when to disengage.

The Role of Parents

As a mentor, you play a very important role in teens' lives. Having a mentor is one of the most effective ways for a young person to stay on track and grow. But you should never underestimate the role of the God-given biological or lawful mentors: the parents. Parents have a tremendous influence in the lives of their children. Failing to recognize their role is an enormous mistake. If you want to maximize the possible impact on your mentees' lives, then you need to be strategic in your relationships with your mentees' parents.

You need to have three practices in your mentoring: 1) Point your mentees to their parents; 2) Support the parents of your mentees in their God-given assignments; 3) Communicate with your mentees' parents when needed.

Sue was a well-liked small group leader. Her girls loved her, and, at the time, so did her girls' parents. At first glance, everyone thought she was an effective and dynamic mentor. But some stress fractures began to appear between some of her mentees and their parents. In fact, parents of three of the four girls she mentored came to me with concerns. They felt that Sue was pulling their girls away from their parental relationships and undermining their authority and the respect their daughters had once had for them. All three families asked me not to let their daughters or Sue know that they talked to me because they were afraid of creating worse strains in their relationships.

I saw signs of the dysfunction myself. I began to have discreet conversations with Sue to probe my growing concerns. What I was able to deduce was that Sue thought her role was more important than that of the parents. She also thought she knew better than the parents. As a result, she undermined the role and influence of the parents in their daughters' lives. Unfortunately, Sue was unteachable and needed to step out of ministry. The damage she caused in her girls' lives left a shadow over the positive investment she made in a three-year period.

Most parents want what is best for their teens, and most parents are trying to do what is right in shepherding their teens. Your role as a mentor is not to hinder parents but to help them. Either through your personal influence or that of your church, you will want to support your mentees' parents and help them be champions. Thinking that we understand or know teens better than their parents is foolish. Today's churches and mentors should be supporting parents, not usurping their authority. Support can also come in the way of creating and equipping supportive ministries that focus on parenting skills development and encouragement. Today's parents need more people in their corner. Today's teens also need more adults in their parents' corner!

117
*

Prayerful Selection

Make sure you are prayerful and selective as you choose your mentees. You have one life to invest. It is important that you take your lead from God on where to invest your time and heart. Failure to do so could cause a missed opportunity to invest in someone else God has chosen for you. The teens I have mentored have been diverse spiritually and socially. Some have been pre-Christian; others have been ministry-minded leaders. Some have been active in sports and academics, and others have been full-time vocational-technical apprentices all through high school. If there was any trait in common, it was their dissatisfaction with their present state and a desire to move forward and grow.

Joe interned with me for four years as a college student. He was a gifted shepherd and emerging teacher. I watched him blossom and mature as a leader in our ministry. Joe wanted to be challenged and mentored to become all that God had for him. His aspiration was to become a youth pastor himself. Whether from wounds or bad experiences, what Joe needed most was confidence. He needed assurance in who he was in Christ and what God wanted to do through him as a servant. He got the experience he needed in his four years of ministry with me. But his confidence issue needed life-on-life mentoring. Joe's coachability was a key ingredient as we sifted through what hindered his confidence and looked to embrace his calling with assurance. Joe had a tender heart and desire to grow. But it took time, affirmation from others, prayer, and the development of a new way of thinking to move him beyond his lack of confidence.

Life-on-life mentoring can only go as far as a mentee is willing to go. As a mentor, you need to prayerfully discern whether you will be able to help your mentees grow based on their desire. We already discussed the importance of your pace in fostering their transformation. A healthy pace and teachability can determine whether you will be able to help those you are considering mentoring. In addition, you may lack certain skills or knowledge to help them move forward. At that point, you can direct them toward other people who may be able to help them. Your role, as a steward of your gifting, is to discern whom you should invest in based on who you are and who the students are.

Make a Plan

A big part of mentoring teens is building relationships. But if your investment in them does not include a challenge to become a better person, then you are selling your mentoring time short. All too often, adults fail to help students grow because they never move beyond simply spending time together and nurturing them.

Life-on-life mentors will challenge mentees to change and grow. They will address difficult issues. For this to occur effectively, it is critical that you periodically set goals with your mentees and revisit them. Failure to do so may leave you both walking in circles. Goal setting gives you a focus and target in mind. Your aim as a mentor is not simply to be a friend or to affirm. While these are important attributes for a mentor, you have to challenge your mentees and help them grow. Goal setting can help you be more effective in fostering their development.

Nick was a born leader. He had influence over his peers in our ministry and on his campus. He was an athlete and creative genius. People followed him. In the six years I had him as a teen, he brought more than one hundred of his peers into our church. What he lacked was patience and the skill set to know how to influence his friends toward personal growth. His lack of patience made him walk away from friendships when he saw character flaws or deficiencies. Rather than being gracious and coaching his friends, he had a tendency to avoid them and walk away. One goal I set with Nick was to help him learn how to coach his peers and influence them toward personal growth. This was a multi-year goal that continues today with check-ins and incremental challenges.

One of Nick's friends, Nate, had an inherent ability to singlehandedly destroy relationships. His neediness and recurring pity parties caused people to avoid him. Nick was at his wit's end with his friend, as were many of his peers. He told me of a time when Nate came to his house to hang out. He asked his parents to tell Nate he was busy, but the truth was that Nick was in the basement with a half dozen of their

119

*

mutual friends. None of the teens at Nick's house wanted to invite Nate in. During our mentoring time, I posed a challenge to Nick: Sit down with Nate and be honest with him. Affirm your commitment to the relationship and then tell him the things he is doing that cause people to avoid him. Nick met with Nate later that week and graciously challenged his friend to change. Today both Nick and Nate are better for it, and I continue to mentor Nick in his interpersonal skills.

Be Flexible

Remember that staying flexible is vital to your mentoring relationship's success. You need to set goals and work toward them. However, life calls for adjustments. If your mentees are going through a crisis, you may need to change the shape of your time together. Discernment and sensitivity should cause you to adjust. You may need to put aside what you intended to cover in a meeting, or over the course of several meetings, and instead spend time listening, praying, and encouraging your mentees on the issues at hand. Life calls for flexibility. Be attentive to what is going on in your mentees' lives. Being a good listener helps you know when you need to change direction permanently, or for a time.

I spent two years mentoring Sarah with a few of her peers in a small-group setting. A lot of our energy focused on helping her become a more effective minister to her high school friends. Through my relationship with Sarah and her parents, it became apparent that some turmoil had arisen at home. For a time, our energy needed to shift. I needed to challenge Sarah in her family relationships. She needed to give attention to strengthening her relationship with her parents and not use peer ministry as an escape from her home. She had loving parents who knew Christ and desired the best for her. But she struggled with some of the natural inclinations of adolescence toward independence and exhibited a lack of respect for her parents in the process. It was time to put aside our peer-to-peer ministry-skill development goal and address Sarah's home life. I met with Sarah once a week for a month and helped her set concrete goals to strengthen her relationships at home. With tough love and a coachable spirit, she was able to see positive changes at home.

Expect Disappointment

When you invest your heart in someone, you are bound to experience disappointment from time to time. Disappointment most often comes when you take your eyes off Christ and place them on your personal expectations. I often find myself guilty of this offense. As a mentor, you need to remember that your mentees are God's work, not yours. You are simply a tool in his hand. God has to be the one to grow them and keep them on track. Sometimes the decisions young people make are disappointing because we see the repercussions when they don't. We want to see them make wise decisions and follow our direction. But some of the time they decide to plot their own course.

I spent three years mentoring Ryan. When we began our friendship, he was a freshman in high school and not a believer. Over the course of a year, he came to Christ, and over the next two years, he demonstrated a desire to mature in his faith and be used by God to influence others. Unfortunately, Ryan gave in to peer pressure that led him down a self-destructive trajectory. Void of a father and living in near impoverished conditions, he lacked direction and healthy self-esteem. These factors probably left him more vulnerable to making the poor decisions he made while spiraling into a life of drugs and withdrawing from his healthy relationships. Repeated attempts to intervene were met with rejection. Today I continue to pray that God will protect him from his dangerous behaviors and bring him back into community with his heavenly Father and the body of Christ.

Beware of Deceit

As a mentor, you will need a discerning spirit. Your mentees may try to misguide or even deceive you at times. The deeper and more insightful your mentoring relationship, the more it will probe into the dark areas of life. Often this can be an awkward and painful experience for mentees. Fear of rejection and judgment, or love for one's sin, can cause deceit to arise as a defense mechanism. In an effort to avoid the place they see you taking them, mentees may fail to be forthright and honest.

Deception may be used when someone is afraid or too attached to a sin or destructive behavior.

As a mentor, knowing when your mentees are being transparent and when they are withholding information or trying to mislead you is an important tool of discernment. For many mentors, this skill only comes with experience. I have been deceived on a number of occasions. Sin has a way of creeping in to people's lives and growing like a cancer that spreads and controls them. When they fail to deal with it, it takes root. Some of the time, mentees may not only deceive you but also themselves.

> . . . but each person is tempted when they are dragged away by their
> own evil desire and enticed. Then, after desire has conceived,
> it gives birth to sin; and sin, when it is full-grown,
> gives birth to death.
> James 1:14-15

Your goal as a mentor is to prayerfully cut through existing deception with God's help. Some of the time, God will give you success. In other instances you may be fooled. From the outside, Ryan appeared to have his act together. But, truth be known, he and his girlfriend became sexually active. They put up a good front at trying to hide their lifestyle, but I was able to discern that something was not right. After a series of meetings with him and his girlfriend—and my observations of them during group settings—I broached the subject. I was repeatedly met with statements of denial. And then, six months later, the truth came out. They had, in fact, been sexually active, and now she was pregnant. As his mentor, I had tried to help him, but he chose instead to entertain a greater desire in his life at the time.

Keep Hope Alive

Although rewarding over the long haul, mentoring can be tough work. It is easy to get discouraged and lose perspective. But hope is always alive when you are involved in God's work. As a mentor, you need to remember that the paths God takes people on do not always go the way you think they should. Some people take long paths before following Jesus with their lives. If you stick with youth work for an extended time, then God will be apt to surprise you more than once. Quite often, when I think the well has run dry, God comes through and does an amazing work in a person's life.

> . . . being confident of this, that he who began a good work in you
> will carry it on to completion until the day of Christ Jesus.
> Philippians 1:6

I have had a few young people I mentored get ensnared in self-destructive lifestyles and walk away from faith in Christ all together. Such experiences are discouraging for mentors. But we must keep hope alive. It is easier to keep a healthy perspective and hold onto hope if we remember who does the work—God, not us.

Recently, I was approached on Facebook by someone I had ministered to twenty years earlier. As I reflected, I remembered him as a teen who professed being a follower of Christ. He was active in our youth ministry and in a small group and had people investing in his life one on one. But then, in his senior year, he began denying his faith and adhering to an agnostic ideology. Now, after twenty years, he contacted me looking for help. God used different circumstances and people to rekindle a flame in him that once burned bright. He was ready to return to his faith in Christ.

Call Others to Join You

You probably know more teens who need mentoring than you can cover yourself. Inviting others to join you as mentors of young people can open the doors for more teens to be impacted by mentoring relationships and for other adults to have the blessing of being used by God in this manner. When you are busy mentoring and doing youth work, your eyes may get focused on what is in front of you, causing you to forget the big picture. But take a moment to pray for God to raise up additional mentors around you, and then invite others to join you.

If you belong to a youth ministry volunteer team, you may consider hosting a brainstorming time to make a list of those in your church who would be good candidates for mentors. There are probably people in your church who, upon hearing your vision and being invited to join you, would gladly invest in a teen's life. Some of these individuals may be adults who were impacted by youth ministry or were mentored as teens. Some may be grandparents or former parents of teens who believe in youth mentoring. The risk of rejection is outweighed by the benefit of being able to find mentors for more teens.

> Then he said to his disciples, "The harvest is plentiful
> but the workers are few. Ask the Lord of the harvest,
> therefore, to send out workers into his harvest field.
> Matthew 9:37-38

Take Time to Evaluate

It is natural to get caught up in life and forget to take time to evaluate. But evaluation is not only helpful; it is necessary for ongoing success in your mentoring relationships. Without evaluation, you may get off course and lose focus on the goals you set out to accomplish. By taking periodic timeouts to evaluate with your mentees, you gain the opportunity to re-center and challenge them forward in the vision of Christlikeness. Reviewing past goals and setting new ones protects your mentoring from becoming ineffective. Your goals should be reviewed every few months and kept in front of you at all times. Mentoring without evaluation is similar to sailing without control of the boat's rudder. Your direction and success are directly linked to your ability to stay on course. Staying on course is more likely when you take time to evaluate.

Don't Try to Change your Mentees

As the mentor, you have more experience in life and an outside perspective that can give you a good vantage point to see where your mentees need to be headed. At times, it can become tempting to try to force them to do what you know is best for them. But you need to remember that you cannot change people. Only God can do that work. While you may be able to manipulate behavior, only God can change hearts. Encouraging change and nudging your mentees to take wise paths is commendable. But you need to pray and allow God to be the one who brings about the lasting change.

Jordan began experimenting with just about every religion one could name. Several people in his life tried to intervene, but he was determined to continue on his chosen path and ignore the wisdom around him. One of his mentors tried heavy-handed apologetics to convince him to change. Although well intentioned, this mentor's tactics backfired, causing Jordan to withdraw and not trust the Christian influencers in his life. At that point Jordan's greatest needs were prayer and friendships with people who would stay connected to him without trying to change him. God is still at work on Jordan. And several people who care about him are hopeful that God will continue to work on his heart.

Keep Growing

It is easy to get into a rut and forget to keep pursuing personal growth, but mentors need to find fresh insights. The moment you stop growing as a mentor is the moment you start taking the road to ineffectiveness. Maintaining the status quo is not an option. We never arrive as servants in this life. Personal growth keeps you sharp and on your game. You can continue your development as a mentor by researching youth culture, attending mentoring seminars, and reading blogs, articles, and books on mentoring. Effective mentors are constant learners. They look for opportunities to grow so they can have a greater influence on the lives of those in whom they invest their hearts.

I have a team of mentors who work with a number of young people in my church. As a team we meet periodically to pray for each other, study mentoring tactics, and sharpen each other through sharing, accountability, and encouragement. Being connected to other mentors is a tangible means toward continued growth. My mentoring counterparts have helped me continue to sharpen my skills as one who invests in teenagers.

Know When to Disengage

Alex grew up in the church and was active in our youth ministry from middle school through his high school graduation. During his high school years, I met with him one on one and in a small group setting a few times a month. Although he seemed to grow throughout the first three years of high school, during his senior year, he began to resist accountability from his friends and advice from me as his mentor. Some of his peer relationships, particularly one with a girl, became unhealthy. Met with repeated resistance and some hostility, I told him that, despite my love for him, it was no longer worth his time or mine to keep meeting. Our agreement was that he had to be as committed to his spiritual walk as I was. But his decisions testified that he was no longer interested in pursuing this endeavor.

I ended our mentoring relationship during his senior year with a caveat. I told him I would begin meeting with him again when he demonstrated a desire to grow through listening to advice from his accountability peers and me. Alex continued to live independent from the Christian influences in his life well into college. We remained in loose contact for a few years, until he asked to meet so we could talk. He apologized for his resistance and said he wanted to get back on course. Alex found a good Christian fellowship at his college and continued to grow in his faith walk with Christ.

Life-on-life mentoring of a teen may be one of the most challenging endeavors you enter into in this life. But it is also undoubtedly one of the most rewarding investments you will ever make. The dividends it pays out to a young person cannot be measured. And the rewards it gives back to you as the mentor are equally great.

Evaluation Questions:

1. Which of the twelve lessons listed in this chapter do you need to give the most attention to in this season of your life?

2. How connected are you to your mentees' parents?

3. What do you do to continue growing as a mentor?

4. How often do you pray for the teens you mentor? Do you have specific ways of praying for them?

5. Have you ever experienced disappointment in a mentoring relationship? How did you deal with it?

Action Steps:

Identify one of the twelve lessons in this chapter as a growth point. Take time to create goals surrounding your area of growth.